Construction of Lugged Bicycle Forks

Marc-Andre R. Chimonas

Logo by Raymond Wang

v1.3 (Content subject to change without notification)

2

Table of Contents

Chapter 1: Introduction

This manual instructs the reader how to build a lugged bicycle fork similar to the one on the front cover. Although the imported mid-level bicycle forks available from bicycle shops and online retailers are affordable and more than adequate for most forms of recreational bicycle riding, building a functional object using your own two hands and simple tools is fun and psychologically rewarding. In our modern times, with specialization and differentiation of labor combined with outsourcing of our manufacturing industries overseas, only a few of us will ever land a job where we get to build something that involves complex multi-step processes. For most people, the sense of achievement that follows the triumph over the inevitable setbacks and frustration inherent to fabrication projects is invaluable. A homemade fork will have value to the creator well beyond a simple material possession.

Content and Objectives

This manual is a companion publication to the book *Lugged Bicycle Frame Construction*. In that manual, I describe how to build a bicycle frame but not a fork. I wrote this book in such a manner as to allow the reader to use this book without ever having read or owned the companion publication. If the reader owns a copy of *Lugged Bicycle Frame Construction*, he will find that content from these two manuals overlaps to some degree.

The fork is the part of the bicycle that connects the frame to the front wheel. A lugged fork, much like a lugged frame, is an assembly of interconnecting metal parts that connect and fit into one another by way of a series of overlapping lugs or sockets. (In this manual, I will use the terms *lugs* and *sockets* interchangeably). The overlap of a lugged metal joint vastly increases the durability of that joint compared to a similar structure assembled without a lug. Lugged bicycle forks, much like lugged bicycle frames, have a high margin of safety and are more forgiving from a technical standpoint to construct than non-lugged forks. From a safety standpoint, minor imperfections in brazing or metal shaping during the construction of a lugged bicycle fork are largely inconsequential (though these errors might affect fork alignment). However, if the reader does a completely hack job, he is destined to make his dentist, orthopedic surgeon, or mortician very rich. By contrast, in lug-less fork construction, even minor errors in arc welding or fillet brazing can lead to catastrophic failures.

In this manual, I will describe the four major skills of lugged fork building, which are the shaping of metal, silver brazing, jigging, and cold setting. I dedicate two chapters to torches and torch brazing. Metal shaping, jigging, and cold setting are covered within the text of the fork-building walkthrough.

Silver brazing is a method of joining pieces of metal together using silver bearing *metallic glue*. Most individuals can learn silver brazing without hands on training. Whereas inexpensive fuel-air torches were sufficient to build some of the bicycle frames described in *Lugged Bicycle Frame Construction*, the more expensive oxy-fuel torch is mandatory for the methods described in this manual. Some of the metal parts of a lugged fork are simply too massive to reach brazing temperature with a $40 fuel-air torch. An oxy-fuel outfit costs several hundred dollars to assemble.

Jigging is a method used to hold metal parts in place during brazing. A synonym for *jig* is *fixture*, and I will use the two terms interchangeable in this manual. I provide the reader with different jigging options.

This manual is broken down into eighteen chapters. Chapters two through eight review general principles of practice and theory, such as fork design, brazing, and the use of torches and other tools. Chapters nine through seventeen are a step-by-step walkthrough of the lugged fork fabrication process. Chapter eighteen contains references.

Pronouns

In this manual, I refer to the builder and reader as *he*. I do not intend to exclude or offend women readers or builders. *He* is a neuter pronoun, and in my opinion *he* reads better than *he or she*.

The Fork Building Candidate

Fork building is not for everyone. Frame and fork building is hard work and can be extremely frustrating at times. Patience is not a virtue in fork building. It is a necessity. Someone looking to learn fork building on his own from a written manual and without hands-on training must first understand how bicycle components fit on a frame and fork and how these components work. This manual assumes the reader is familiar with the following bicycle components: headsets, hubs, axles, rims, forks, cranks, pedals, seat posts, saddles, derailleurs, shifters, brake calipers, brake levers, stems, and handlebars.

The ideal fork-building candidate should be able to build up a complete bicycle from bare frame and unassembled components. At a bare minimum, the reader should be able to remove and install a fork, easily tune mechanical derailleurs and brakes, and effectively true a wheel.

Safety

Building a bicycle fork opens the door to a large set of potential hazards. Welders and metal fabricators have much higher rates of occupational illness and injury than your typical overpaid office potato. Even small hand held power tools can devitalize human flesh rapidly. Some brazing rods contain cadmium, which can cause kidney failure, bone loss, emphysema, lung cancer, and other serious illnesses. Heat applied to zinc-containing brazing rods can release zinc oxide fumes, which can cause metal fume fever. Brazing fluxes contain halogens and all sorts of nasty poisons that should not be eaten, inhaled, or absorbed though the skin. A poorly built fork can fail, causing the rider to wreck and sustain injury. Acetylene gas is inherently unstable and can ignite without an ignition source. Builders using torches carelessly can cause fires and subsequent property damage, injury, or death. The list of things that could go wrong goes on and on and on. Realistically, I cannot point out every possible hazard to the reader. Ultimately the fork builder is responsible for his own safety.

The best safety advice I can give the reader is:

> 1. Be careful and mindful of your surroundings.

2. Learn about the properties of the products you plan to use. Obtain manufacturer's safety data sheets (MSDS) from the manufacturer.

3. When using torches, place a charged fire extinguisher within reach.

4. Read the manual and safety precautions for every piece of equipment you buy, borrow, or use.

5. Wear the correct personal protective equipment (PPE) recommended by MSDS and user manuals.

6. Do not attempt fork building while distracted, tired, or under the influence of drugs or alcohol.

7. Perform all brazing, cutting, cleaning, and grinding in a well-ventilated area.

If the builder follows these seven safety tips, he will reduce his chances of an accident but not completely eliminate all risk. Unfortunately, there are no guarantees in life. Even if the builder strictly follows all the directions in this book, he still risks injury or death from the fork building process or from subsequent fork failure. The author, editors, and any other entity associated with the printing, distribution, or sale of this book do not accept any responsibility or liability for injury or death that may become the reader or builder.

Metric Units

For the sake of brevity and to eliminate confusion I use the metric system almost exclusively throughout this manual. I feel that metric measurements are more precise than the English System and that base ten units create less confusion and error than changing denominators with every subsequent mark on a linear scale. I have retained a few English units for temperatures, pressures, and for items commonly sold in English units in the US (such as 1/16" brazing rods). A reader who desires English units for linear measurements can perform his own metric to English conversions using the formula: 1" = 25.4mm.

Final Thoughts

Some fork terminology is well standardized throughout the bicycle industry. Other terminology has not been well standardized, meaning two builders might use the same term differently. I preface non-standardized terminology with the phrase, "in this manual, we will call..." or something similar.

Lastly, I wrote this book as a *how-to* manual and not as a desk reference where items are looked up on an as-needed basis. To be successful, you must read every word of this manual except chapters and sections labeled as *optional*.

Chapter 2: Review of Bicycle Frame Nomenclature

The bicycle frame and fork are two interconnected parts that do not function independently from one another. The frame-fork combination determines the ride characteristics of the bicycle, not just the fork or the frame by itself. In this chapter, we review the parts and angles of a bicycle frame so that we can later describe how the frame and fork interact to produce a characteristic ride quality.

Tube Nomenclature and Frame Angles

Figure 2-1 illustrates the tubes, angles, and other features of the bicycle. This figure contains abbreviations that are defined in the text below. We will use these abbreviations throughout the remainder of this manual. The right side of the bicycle is where the chainrings, chain, and sprockets are located and is, therefore, called the *drive side* of the frame. The left side is the *non-drive side*.

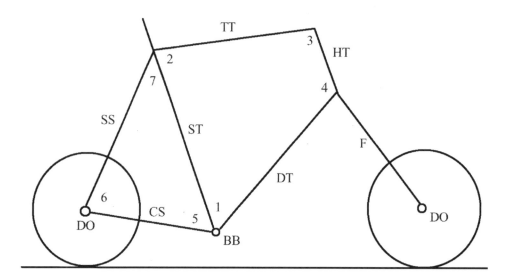

Figure 2-1: *Tubes and angle of a bicycle frame. Letters refer to tubes or other frame parts. Numbers refer to angles.*

Metallic Parts

BB = Bottom bracket shell. The bottom bracket cartridge, cranks, and pedals all connect here. The bottom bracket shell is a short tube oriented perpendicular to the long axis (length) of the bicycle frame.

ST = Seat tube. The seat post and saddle insert into the top of the seat tube. The seat tube length is the main determinant of the height of the bike. A rider with short legs needs a frame with a short seat tube.

TT = Top tube. The top tube usually runs parallel to the ground (classic geometry) or slants upwards. The top tube length is the main determinant of the length of the bike. A rider with long arms or a long torso needs a frame with a long top tube.

DT = Down tube. The length of the down tube helps to determine *front center* (discussed later).

HT = Head tube. Headset cups insert at both ends. The fork and front wheel are below, and the cockpit with handlebars and stem are above.

The seat tube, top tube, down tube, head tube, and bottom bracket shell compose the front triangle of the bicycle. (Of course, the front triangle is a misnomer because the structure is a quadrilateral with four sides and not three). All four true angles of the front triangle (angles 1, 2, 3, and 4) add up to 360 degrees.

F = Fork. The fork connects the front wheel to the frame. The steering tube of the fork inserts into the headset and head tube. At the bottom of the fork are the front dropouts that hold the front wheel.

SS = Seat stay. There are two, one on each side of the rear wheel. The stay stays are usually bridged with a brake bridge or stiffener.

CS = Chain stay. There are two, one on each side of the rear wheel.

DO = Dropout. Dropouts are placed at the intersection of the chain stays and seat stays and at the ends of the fork blades. The dropouts hold the wheels in place. For the purposes of this manual, we will use the term *slot* to refer to the opening in the dropout where the wheel axle is placed.

The rear dropouts, chain stays, seat stays, and bottom bracket shell compose the rear triangle. (Actually there are two rear triangles, one on either side of the rear wheel, but we refer to them as if there were only one). The angles of each triangle (angles 5, 6, and 7) add up to 180 degrees.

Frame Angles

1 = Seat tube–down tube (ST-DT) angle.

2 = Seat tube–top tube (ST-TT) angle.

3 = Top tube–head tube (TT-HT) angle.

4 = Down tube–head tube (DT-HT) angle. Note that, in reality, this angle is obtuse meaning that the angle is greater than 90 degrees. However, frame-building supply vendors measure this angle as if it were acute (less than 90 degrees) by subtracting the true angle from 180 degrees. So a DT-HT angle measured with a protractor as 120 degrees is called by vendors "a 60 degree DT-HT angle." In this manual we will only use the true, obtuse measurement.

5 = Seat tube-chain stay (ST-CS) angle.

6 = Chain stay-seat stay (CS-SS) angle.

7 = Seat tube-seat stay (ST-SS) angle.

Not shown in Figure 2-1 are the chain stay–chain stay (CS-CS) angle and the seat stay–seat stay (SS-SS) angle. The CS-CS angle is measured as half of the angle between the chain stays. For example, a frame with chain stays that form a 14-degree angle relative to one another is called a "7 degree CS-CS angle." The SS-SS angle has little importance in fork design.

Frame angles remain the same regardless of our approach or point of view. Hence, the ST-TT angle is the same as the TT-ST angle. In this manual, we will use different expressions of the same angle (such as ST-DT and DT-ST) interchangeably. We will also refer to the *CS-DT angle* as the sum of the adjacent CS-ST and ST-DT angles.

Other Important Measurements

Several parameters critical to fork and frame design cannot be directly measured along the metal parts of a frame and fork. The dashed lines in Figure 2-2 represent the imaginary lines we use to measure more abstract parameters.

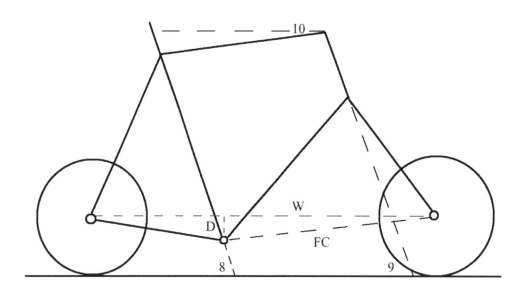

Figure 2-2: *Dashed lines represent imaginary lines. Letters represent linear distances, and numbers represent angles.*

W = Wheelbase. Wheelbase is traditionally defined as the distance between the two points where the two wheels touch the ground. In this manual, we assume the front and rear wheels have the same outer diameter, so we can also define wheelbase as the horizontal distance between the centers of the front and rear dropouts. Furthermore, our assumption of equal wheel diameters means W in Figure 2-2 is parallel to the ground. Bicycles with short wheelbases are capable of tighter turns than bicycles with longer wheelbases. However, under most circumstances wheelbase is a rather minor determinant of a bicycle's handling characteristics compared to fork trail (discussed in the next chapter).

FC = Front center. Front center is the distance between the center of the bottom bracket shell and the center of the front dropouts. If front center is short, the rider may experience problems with *toe overlap*, meaning his toes can contact the front wheel when he steers.

D = Bottom bracket drop. D is the vertical displacement of the center of the bottom bracket shell measured downward from W in Figure 2-2 (because W is parallel to the ground). The vertical distance between the center of the bottom bracket shell and ground is known as the *bottom bracket height.*

8 = Seat angle. The seat angle is the angle of the seat tube relative to the ground. This angle does not influence the handling characteristics of the bicycle nearly as much as the head angle. Another name for seat angle is *seat tube angle.*

9 = Head angle. The head angle is the angle of the head tube relative to the ground. This angle is a determinant of fork trail, which has a major influence on the handling characteristics of the bicycle. Another name for head angle is *head tube angle.*

10 = Top tube slope. Top tube slope is the angle of the top tube measured relative to the ground. In *classic geometry* this angle is zero. A positive angle means that the top tube slopes upward along its span toward the front of the bicycle, and a negative angle means the top tube slopes downward. In Figure 2-2, our top tube slope is positive.

Chapter 3: Structure of the Lugged Bicycle Fork

Fork Parts

A lugged bicycle fork consists of a steering tube, fork crown, two fork blades, two dropouts, and two optional brake bosses for cantilever brakes. Figure 3-1 shows these parts prior to assembly. Figure 17-2 (Chapter 17) shows these same fork parts after assembly and painting.

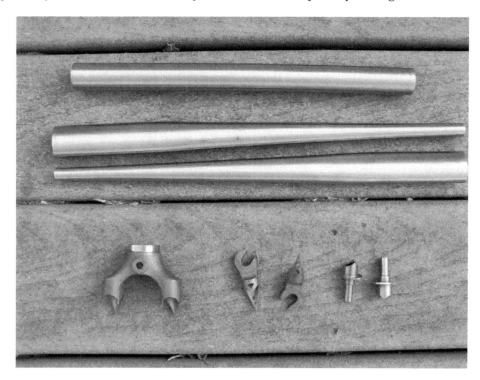

Figure 3-1: *Parts of the bicycle frame prior to assembly: The steering tube (unthreaded) is at the top of the picture; two fork blades are below the steering tube; the fork crown is in the lower left corner; dropouts (socketed) are to the right of the crown; brake bosses (optional) for cantilever brakes are in the lower right corner.*

The Steering Tube

Another name for the steering tube is the *steerer*. The steering tube inserts into the head tube of the bicycle frame. Bearings inside the headset cups allow the steering tube to rotate smoothly. The outer diameter of the cross section of the steering tube is typically 25.4 mm or 28.6 mm. The 28.6 mm steering tube is a relatively modern invention, becoming popular in the 1990s. The 25.4 mm steering tube dates back over 100 years. More recent innovations, including steering tubes as thick as 38.1 mm and tapering outer tube diameters, generally do not fit into lugged crowns. A steering tube can be threaded or threadless for use with threaded or threadless headsets, respectively.

The threads of a threaded steering tube occur at the tube's top end. Production forks usually have a vertical grove or *keyway* cut into the threads to eliminate rotation of headset spacers and the cable hanger. The keyway is typically oriented at the back of the steering tube, facing the rider. The keyway also allows the use of a keyed washer when assembling the bicycle's headset. The keyed washer allows the rider to use a single wrench when adjusting the headset. Most threaded steering tubes available from frame and fork building supply retailers do not come with a keyway. Novice builders should not attempt to cut their own keyway using a file or other simple hand tools or they will risk ruining the threads. Rather, novice builders should simply acquire a threaded headset that allows two wrenches for adjustment.

Most threaded and unthreaded steering tubes are *butted*, meaning the metal wall of the tube is thicker at one end than at the other. The *butted end* is the end with the thicker metal wall and narrower inner diameter. The butted end increases the durability of the fork and is placed into the fork crown, a location of high mechanical stress.

The Fork Crown

A lugged fork crown (Figure 3-2) connects the steering tube to the fork blades. The crown is a three-dimensional structure with height, width, and length. For the purposes of this manual, we will call the imaginary line that runs up and down the height of the crown and steering tube the *vertical axis*. We will call the imaginary line that runs through the width of the crown and connects the tops of the two fork blades the *wide axis*. We will call the imaginary line that runs from the front of the crown towards the back the *short axis*.

Figure 3-2: *A lugged fork crown. The front faces the reader. The crown race and steering tube socket are up top. The points of the fork blade sockets are at the bottom. This particular fork crown is sloped, meaning the tops of the fork blade sockets lie below the top of the crown.*

The round metal ring at the top of the fork is called the *crown race*. The *race ring* of the headset fits here. To allow the headset race ring to fit properly, the builder usually has to mill down the outside diameter of the fork crown race.

For the purposes of this manual, the large round socket at the top of the crown (inside the crown race) is the *steering tube socket*, which allows insertion of the steering tube. The steering tube sockets of most fork crowns are cast to tight tolerances, allowing a good, tight drop-in fit of the steering tube without the need for grinding or machining. Many crowns have a steering tube socket with a small lip or ledge at the bottom to prevent the steering tube from protruding all the way through the bottom of the crown. Some crowns have steering tube sockets with an unchanging bore diameter.

In this manual, we will call the two smaller sockets at the bottom of the fork crown *the fork blade sockets*, which allow insertion of the fork blades. The inner contours and cross sectional measurements of the fork blade sockets must correspond to the outer contours and measurements of the fork blades. Otherwise, the fork blades will not fit properly. The fork blade sockets of most fork crowns are cast to loose tolerances, meaning appropriately sized fork blades are not always a drop-in fit. Grinding out the sockets or reshaping (pinching) the blades is often necessary. The bottom ends of the fork blade sockets usually end in *points*. Fork part retailers often provide a linear distance called *wheel clearance*. Wheel clearance is measured between the outer surfaces of the insides of the two fork blade sockets parallel to the wide axis of the crown. The wheel clearance needs to be at least 5 mm wider than the width of the desired tire. Larger differences (1 cm or more) between wheel clearance and tire width are needed if the rider intends to ride under muddy conditions.

A fork crown in which the tops of the fork blade sockets (shoulders) lie in line with the top of the crown is called a *flat top* fork crown. A fork crown in which the tops of the fork blade sockets are placed below the top of the crown is called a *sloped crown* (Figure 3-2). There are several sub-varieties of sloped crown including *full slope* and *partial slope*.

Most fork crowns have fork blade sockets that run (more or less) parallel to the crown's vertical axis (and the steering tube). Some crowns have fork blades sockets tilted forward or *offset* 6 or 7 degrees relative to the vertical axis (Figure 3-3). The fork blades for such crowns do not need bending to achieve *fork rake* (described later). In this manual, we will call a fork with a 6 or 7 degree offset crown a *straight bladed fork*. Such forks are among the easiest to fabricate and are highly recommended for the first time fork builder. Bending fork blades properly can be tricky.

Henry James makes a crown with fork blade sockets offset 3 degrees relative to the steering tube. These crowns are intended for blades with a smaller than usual bend but not completely straight. In this manual, Chapter 12: Bending Fork Blades describes how to create rake relative to the large end of the fork blade. Crowns with 3 degree offset require building rake relative to the steering tube, which is not explicitly described in this manual.

Caliper brakes mount to the fork through holes at the front and back of the crown. Some crowns come with the holes pre-drilled. Others do not. These holes are useful during the fork construction process, specifically during brazing. Even if the rider does not intend to use caliper-type brakes, the holes in the crown can serve as a mount for other bicycle parts such as fenders.

Figure 3-3: *A straight bladed fork. This particular fork design, with socketed dropouts, is probably among the easiest forks to fabricate.*

Fork Blades

Fork blades (Figures 3-1, 3-3) run along the sides of the wheel and connect the fork crown to the front dropouts. At the time of purchase, fork blades are typically 380 to 400 mm long. For the purposes of this manual, we will call the imaginary line that runs lengthways through the center of the fork blades the *long axis*. For the vast majority of lugged forks, the fork blades splay outward as they run downward, meaning the distance between the long axes of the two fork blades is smaller at the crown than at the dropouts.

In lugged forks, the two ends of a fork blade have different cross sectional diameters. We will call the end with the smaller cross sectional diameter, the *small end*. The small end is usually circular with an outer diameter of 12.5 mm. The dropouts attach at the small ends.

We will call the end of the fork blade with the larger cross sectional area the *large end*. The large ends insert into the fork blade sockets of the crown. Most fork blades have large ends with an oval cross section. The long axis of the oval is typically 28 mm long and the short axis is typically 20 mm long. The short axes of the blades' large end cross sections run parallel to the wide axis of the crown to provide more wheel clearance. Some fork blades have large ends with round cross sections. The outer diameter of round large ends is typically 24 or 25.4 mm. Blades with round large ends are usually intended for track bicycles with narrow tires. Round blades are easier to bend than oval blades because the radial symmetry of a round blade allows a simple correction of a bend that bows out to the side (Chapter 12). Another subset of fork blades have large ends with teardrop-shaped cross sections. Such blades are typically called *aero blades*. The point of the teardrop occurs at the back of the blade. When planning a fork build, the shape and outer measurements of the large end of the fork blades must correspond to the shape and inner measurements of the fork blade sockets of the crown.

The portion of the fork blade where the outside measurements of the cross section transition from those of the large end to those of the small end is the *tapering section* or *taper* (Figures 3-1, 3-3). The taper usually occurs over a length of 290mm along the long axis of the blade.

Fork blades generally do not have uniform wall thicknesses. The large end usually has a wall thickness between 0.6 to 1.0 mm. The small end usually has a wall thickness between 0.9 to 1.8mm. Thinner walled fork blades are easier to bend when creating fork rake (discussed below). Thicker walled fork blades make a fork somewhat stiffer and less supple.

Fork blades are typically bent to create a *rake*. Rake is a critical component of *fork trail*, a parameter that influences the steering qualities of a bicycle. We will discuss rake and trail in the next chapter. Some manufacturers, such as Reynolds Technology, fabricate fork blades that are already bent for the builder. Such blades usually come in either 30 mm or 45 mm rakes. Pre-bent blades will save the builder much effort because bending fork blades properly using a homemade mandrel can be difficult.

Once a fork blade is bent to create rake, we no longer have a liner structure. For a bent blade, we will refer to the *long axis of the small end* and the *long axis of the large end* as being distinct and separate.

Dropouts

The front dropouts connect at the small ends of the fork blades and are the anchor points for the front wheel. Dropouts can be socketed, plugged, or forged from flat stock. Many dropouts have small lips on their outer surfaces to secure the outer locknuts of the wheel axle or the locking mechanism of the quick release skewer (Figure 3-1). Frame builders often refer to these lips pejoratively as *lawyer tabs*.

Socketed dropouts, as the name implies, have sockets that slip over the small ends of the fork blades (Figures 3-1, 3-3). The inner diameter of the socket must correspond to the outer diameter of the small end of the fork blade. Socketed dropouts are by far the easiest dropouts to use in fork construction, requiring little or no reshaping of metal to properly fit around the fork blade. Unfortunately, few socketed dropouts come with eyes for mounting racks or fenders.

Plugged dropouts, as the name implies, have a plug that inserts inside the hole at the small end of the fork blade. The outer diameter of the plug must correspond roughly (within 0.5 mm) to the inner diameter of the small end of the fork blade. At the bottom of a plug is a protruding lip. The outer diameter of the lip should be the same size as, or bigger than, the outer diameter of the small end of the fork blade. The wall thicknesses of the small ends of fork blades vary much from one manufacturer to the next, and from one production run to the next for a single manufacturer. Plugs seldom fit the inner diameters of fork blades as well as sockets of socketed dropouts fit the outer diameters. Most manufacturers of plugged dropouts warn the builder that grinding or sleeving the plugs may be necessary. For these reasons plugged dropouts are more difficult to use than socketed dropouts. However, many plugged dropouts are cast with eyes to mount racks or fenders.

Dropouts forged or cut from flat stock require a builder to cut slots into the small ends of his fork blades. Compared to fitting socketed or plugged dropouts, slotting fork blades is a complicated process involving many steps that require precision and allow the possibility for much error. Therefore, dropouts from flat stock are not covered in this manual, which is intended for the novice builder.

Most front wheels have front axels that measure 9 mm in diameter. Many of the procedures of this manual require a threaded rod as a type of jig. Threaded 9 mm rods are uncommon. The builder will likely have to use a 3/8" rod which is 9.5 mm in metric units. Sometimes 3/8" rods fit front dropouts well. Other times the builder will need to enlarge the slot slightly with a file.

Brake Bosses (Optional)

Brake bosses (Figures 3-1, 3-3) anchor cantilever brake calipers (including linear pull V-brake calipers) to the fork blades. Brake bosses are not required if the builder does not intend to use cantilever brakes. The base of brake bosses can be flat or *mitered*. A miter is a curved contour that more or less matches the contour of the front of the fork blade. Mitered brake bosses will save the builder considerable time and effort at (usually) no added expense.

A cantilever brake caliper's point of attachment is the cylinder that protrudes from the front of the boss. These cylinders are threaded internally for mounting bolts. The cylinder is often offset a few millimeters towards the midline of the fork relative to the mitered mounting surface of the base. Unless the builder chooses a very wide crown, a shorter offset (0 to 7 mm) works best.

Most brake bosses have one to three small holes at the front of the base. These holes allow insertion of the end of the brake caliper's tensioning spring. The vast majority of cantilever and V-brakes require these holes. Three holes allow greater adjustability in spring tension than one hole.

Disc Tabs

Disc brakes have become very popular. Although discs are necessary for gravity sports such as mountain bike downhill and freeride, caliper or cantilever brakes are usually adequate for most other cycling disciplines including cyclocross and cross country mountain biking. Most fork blades manufactured for lugged fork construction are too narrow, thin walled, and supple to permit the use of disc brakes (Figure 3-4). Furthermore, most fork crowns are too flexible to handle the torque and leverage created by disc brakes. Mounting a disc brake on a lugged fork may result in brake chatter, fork fatigue, and fork failure. Disc tabs are, therefore, not recommended for novice builders and for most lugged forks for that matter.

Figure 3-4: *Fork blades from two different road forks from the same manufacturer. Note that the fork blade with the disc tab (right) is fatter than the other fork blade, which was not built for disc brakes. The fork blades and crowns typically used in classic lugged forks cannot withstand the forces generated by disc brakes.*

Fork Materials

In the last few decades, we have witnessed the introduction of new composite materials and exotic metals into the field of cycling. Unfortunately, the methods presented in this manual cannot be used effectively or safely with carbon fiber or non-ferrous metals such as aluminum, titanium, beryllium, scandium, magnesium, mithril, adamantium, or unobtainium. The reader of this manual is limited to the iron-base metals described below. Though less popular these days among consumers and manufactures of mass-produced frames and forks, ferrous materials yield bicycles with excellent ride characteristics by providing just the right amount of flexibility, stiffness, and vibration damping.

Mild Steel

Mild steel is comprised almost entirely of iron, with a very small amount (<0.3%) of carbon. Mild steel is inexpensive, and is suitable for dropouts, frame lugs, bottom bracket shells, fork crowns, and tubes and stays drawn with thick walls. Mild steel cannot be effectively hardened or strengthened by heat treatment. Frame and fork parts made from mild steel are generally heavy because the relatively low toughness of mild steel does not permit thin-walled structures.

Chromoly

Chromoly (CRMO) is a group of tough, low alloy steels that contain trace amounts (<2% each) of the metallic elements chromium, molybdenum, and manganese. The toughness of CRMO allows tubes, stays, and other parts to have thinner walls and less mass than similar structures drawn or cast from mild steel. 4130 series chromoly works very well for all bicycle and fork parts and is the frame material of choice for the novice frame and fork builder. Some formulations of chromoly can be heat treated, quenched, tempered, and/or annealed resulting in very hard, thin walled, light, and stiff frame and fork parts. However, prolonged overheating during brazing or welding alters steel's granular structure, reversing the effects of some categories of heat treatments. Heat treated steels are, therefore, not recommended for novice builders who are new to brazing and likely to overheat steel parts.

Austenitic Stainless Steel

Austenitic stainless steels, such as 304 and 316 series stainless steels, have a high content of chromium (>15%) and nickel (>8%). Austenitic stainless steels cannot be hardened through heat treatments but can be toughened by cold working. Most forms of austenite have a high tensile strength but are brittle and prone to cracking. Austenitic steels are used in dropouts, frame lugs, bottom bracket shells, and fork crowns. Frame builders generally regard 304 and 316 series stainless as inadequate for use as frame tubes (other than the head tube), stays, and fork blades. Reynolds 921 is a cold worked austenitic steel tough enough for use as a fork blade. All stainless steels have thermal properties that predispose them to warping and deforming if heated unevenly. Prolonged heating of austenitic stainless steels can result in carbide precipitation, an alteration of the granular structure that weakens the metal and predisposes to corrosion. Austenitic stainless steels are, therefore, not recommended for novice builders

Martensitic Stainless Steels

Martensitic stainless steels, such as 410 and 420 series stainless steels, KVA stainless, Columbus XCR, and Reynolds 953, have lower nickel content than austenitic steels and are invariably hardened and strengthened by heat treatment. Unlike most austenitic stainless steels, martensite allows for tough, thin walled, and light frame tubes, stays, and fork blades. Martensitic stainless steels are cheaper than titanium but are more expensive than chromoly. Much like austenitic stainless, martensitic steels are prone to warping when heated unevenly and are, therefore, not recommended for the first time builder. Furthermore, prolonged over heating can reverse some of the strengthening effects of heat treatment. When brazed with zinc-containing brazing alloys, martensitic stainless steels are prone to crevice corrosion whereby the brazing alloy detaches from the steel over time when exposed to high humidity or aquatic environments. Crevice corrosion is likely a non-issue with cycling applications unless the bicycle is severely neglected or abused.

Other Forms of Stainless Steel

Precipitation alloys, such as Reynolds 931, are similar to martensitic steels and are used for bicycling applications. Duplex and ferritic stainless steels are not used for cycling applications.

Ordering Parts, a Checklist

The following is a list of questions the reader should answer to make sure his fork parts fit together properly:

1. If you are a novice builder, are all fork parts made from either mild steel or chromoly?
2. Is the outer diameter of the steering tube appropriate for your headset and head tube?
3. Does your headset require a threaded or threadless steering tube?
4. Does the steering tube socket of your crown match the outer diameter of your steering tube?
5. Does the steering tube socket of your crown have a lip to prevent the steering tube from protruding through the bottom?
6. If you do not want to bend your fork blades, are the fork blade sockets of the crown offset 6 or 7 degrees forward relative to the steering tube?
7. Will the distance between the insides of the fork blade sockets of the crown provide adequate wheel clearance for your choice of tire?
8. Do the large ends of the fork blades have a cross section with the same shape and dimensions as the inner contours of the crown's fork blade sockets?
9. Will the fork blades be long enough for your intended crown-to-axle length (discussed in the next chapter)?
10. Will you be using plugged or socketed dropouts?
11. Do you need eyes on your dropouts to mount a fender or rack?
12. Is the inner diameter of the socket of the dropout the same as the outer diameter of the small end of the fork blade?
13. Is the outer diameter of the plug of the dropout (more or less) the same as the inner diameter of the small end of the fork blade?
14. Do you need brake bosses for cantilever brakes?
15. Is the offset of the brake boss too large?
16. Is the base of the brake boss mitered?
17. Are there small holes in the brake boss for the end of the caliper's tension spring?
18. Are the fork parts compatible with your fork design and your fork's intended use (Chapter 4)?

Chapter 4: The Function of the Bicycle Fork, Design Considerations

In this chapter, and the one that follows, we describe how design parameters and features of a fork influence a bicycle's handing and ride characteristics. The emphasis of this chapter is on qualitative effects, meaning the *general feel* of the fork-frame combination. The target measurements provided in the table of this chapter work quite well to construct a fully functioning fork with handling characteristics appropriate to a general classification of bicycle (road racing, cyclocross, etc.). The following chapter, Quantitative Fork Design, provides a mathematical model based on trigonometric functions to enhance the precision of a fork build and to allow fine-tuning of bicycle handling.

Crown-to-Axle Length

Crown-to-axle length, as used in this manual, is the distance from the top of the crown, measured right below the crown race, to a point along the fork's midline equidistant to the centers of the two dropout slots. Crown-to-axle length is synonymous with the length of a fork. Increasing crown-to-axle length, while holding all other frame and fork parameters constant, has the following effects:

1. Raises the bottom bracket height, providing more downward toe clearance but less stand-over clearance.
2. Increases front center providing less toe overlap (and more clearance).
3. Decreases the head angle.

Mathematical formulae to quantify the effects of 1 through 3 above are described in the next chapter. As a crude rule of thumb, a 1 cm increase in crown-to-axle length decreases the head angle by approximately 0.5 degrees. The effects of head angle on handling are described below.

Fork Rake and Mechanical Trail

Trail is defined as the distance between the point where the wheel contacts the ground and the point where an imaginary line drawn through the steering axis (head tube) contacts the ground (Figure 4-1). Trail has a major influence on the handling characteristics of a bicycle, but trail does not act alone. A frame's wheelbase, bottom bracket height, and the angular momentum of the wheel (which is a function of wheel size, tire weight, etc.) also influence how quickly a bicycle can turn. As a general rule of thumb, longer trail (>70 mm) results in stable, more sluggish steering, and shorter trail (<60 mm) results in faster, twitchy steering. However, there are two notable exceptions to this rule: strong cross winds and weight-loaded handlebars. (We discuss these exceptions in more detail below).

Forks are usually built with a *rake* (aka *fork offset*) to decrease trail. Rake is defined as the forward displacement of the dropouts relative to the steering axis line (Figure 4-1, right). The builder can achieve fork rake by either bending the fork blades forward or by selecting a fork crown that angles the fork blades forward (usually about 6 or 7 degrees). A builder could even build a fork with negative trail, meaning the wheel contacts the ground in front of the steering axis. In most circumstances, such a frame and fork combination would feel very unstable. *Camber* is the extent of the bend in the blade. The higher location of the bend along the fork blade, the less camber required to achieve a target fork rake.

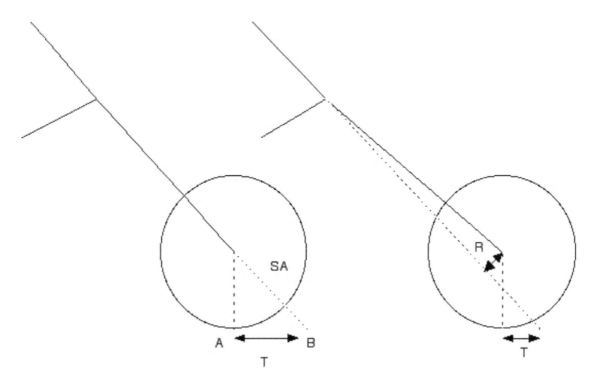

Figure 4-1: *In this figure, the two frames have the same wheel diameter and head angle. SA = steering axis (an imaginary line); A = point of wheel contact to ground; B = point where steering axis contacts ground; T = trail; R = rake. The fork on the left has no rake, so the dropouts lie along the same line as the steering axis. The fork on the right has been moved forward from the steering axis with a rake, shortening the trail. The frame and fork combination on the right has a shorter trail and will, therefore, steer tighter and handle faster than the one on the left.*

Trail can be predicted through the mathematical formula:

$$Trail = \frac{wheel\ radius \times cosine\ (head\ angle) - rake}{sine\ (head\ angle)}$$

According to this formula, increasing wheel radius increases trail, and increasing rake decreases trail. The typical range of head angles for most bicycles is between 69 to 74 degrees. Increasing the head angle within this range results in shorter trail.

Conspicuously absent from the formula above is crown-to-axle length. Crown-to-axle length effects trail indirectly, however, by influencing head angle. Indeed, the formula above has utility to determine trail only once a frame and fork have already been fabricated and assembled. The rider can measure his head angle and simply plug and chug his numbers into the equation. However, used alone, this formula cannot accurately predict trail during the planning stages of frame and fork construction when many frame and fork parameters have yet to be determined. When designing a fork and frame, trail is often an important outcome variable, and frame and fork parameters such as crown-to-axle length and HT-DT angle are selected based on their effects on fork trail. The interaction between the frame and fork parameters that directly and indirectly result in fork trail is complex, requiring multiple mathematical equations and not just one. These formulae are provided in the next chapter.

Conditions When Short Trail Predict Stable Handling

Strong crosswinds apply a sideways force to the front wheel. Trail acts as a type of lever arm for this force. The wheel of a bicycle with short trail will deflect less with such a force than a bicycle with longer trail. Therefore, in strong crosswinds, bicycles with shorter trail will feel more stable than bicycles with longer trail.

Wheel flop is the downward movement of the front end of a bicycle when the front wheel is steered from zero (straight ahead) to ninety degrees. Mathematically, we can express wheel flop as follows:

Flop = trail x sine (head angle) x cosine (head angle)

Wheel flop is important when a heavy load is placed on the handlebars. By heavy load, we mean loads typical of a porteur bicycle such as a full jug of milk (> 3 kg) and not simply a map or windbreaker in a handlebar bag. If flop is large, weight on the handlebars will gravitate downhill creating a tendency for the bars to move sideways and the bicycle to steer spontaneously. The rider will have to apply significant torque to move the load on the handlebars uphill to center the steering. According to our formula above, flop increases as trail increases. Therefore, bicycles designed for heavy front-end loads, such as porteur bicycles, will be more stable with shorter trail. Trail for porteur bicycles is typically around 30mm, requiring a larger fork rake around 65mm.

Parameters of Production Forks

Table 4-1 lists head angle, wheel and tire size, crown-to-axle length, rake, and trail typical of mass produced forks based on cycling discipline. A builder who fears math and wishes to avoid the calculations in the next chapter can use this table as a rough guideline to design a fork. For example, let us pretend that a builder wishes to build a fork for his cyclocross frame, only he wants his bicycle to handle tighter than a typical production bicycle. He can start with the given production values of 400 mm and 45 mm for crown-to-axle length and rake, respectively. To make the bicycle more nimble, he could either decrease the crown-to-axle length (to increase head angle) or increase the rake by about 1 cm. Either method (or both) would result in decreased fork trail. Large departures from the crown-to-axle length and rake values on Table 4-1 are not recommended unless the builder performs the calculations in the next chapter to verify the resulting trail is not extreme. Absent from this table are the special cases of porteur bicycle forks (discussed above) and rigid cross country mountain bike forks (discussed below).

Bicycle Type	Head Angle	Rim(ISO)	Tire	C-A	Rake	Trail	Steering
road racing 700c	73	622	23	370	45	55	tight
tri/time trial 650c	72	571	23	350	45	53	tight
touring 700c	72	622	32	390	45	64	relaxed
touring 650b	71	584	32	385	45	64	relaxed
touring 26"	71	559	38	375	45	62	relaxed
cyclocross 700c	72	622	32	400	45	64	relaxed
track/fixie 700c	74	622	23	370	38	56	tight

Table 4-1: *Fork parameters for production bicycles based on cycling application. All numbers other than head angle are in mm. Head angle may vary + or – up to 1 degree based on frame size and manufacturer preferences. ISO rim sizes are well standardized with negligible variance. The suggested tire sizes (width) are not mandatory but were used to estimate fork trail. Crown-to-axle length (C-A) may vary + or – up to 10 mm between manufacturers. Rake may vary + or - up to 5 mm between manufacturers. Trail may vary + or – up to 5 mm (or even more) based on the variance of other parameters.*

Flex and Shock Absorption

In addition to determining the steering and handling qualities of a bicycle, the fork plays a significant role in shock absorption. A fork's flexibility determines the ability to dampen vibrations and road bumps. Flexible, supple forks dampen bumps and vibrations well and are desirable for long rides on improved roads. Stiff forks do not dampen bumps or vibrations well but provide more efficient rides during racing. Stiff forks are less likely to fail under harsh riding conditions such as prolonged use on dirt roads, poor roads with potholes, or single track.

The major determinants of fork flex are the length, the average outer diameter, and the wall thickness of the fork blades. The extent of the bend in the fork blade and the location of the bend are rather minor determinant of fork flex compared to other fork parameters.

Longer fork blades flex more than shorter fork blades. A builder who wishes to effectively minimize the length of his fork blades while preserving his desired crown-to-axle length should select a fork crown with sloping shoulders. Compared to a flat top fork crown, a sloping crown places the tops of the fork blade sockets downward a few centimeters.

The reader may recall that fork blades have both large and small ends. The majority of fork blades need to be cut down to size for most target crown-to-axle lengths. By cutting from the large end, the builder effectively creates a fork blade that has a smaller average outer diameter throughout its length. Such fork blades make for supple, flexible forks. By cutting from the small end, the builder effectively creates a fork blade that has a larger average outer diameter. Such fork blades make for rigid, more efficient forks.

All other factors being equal, fork blades with thicker wall thicknesses are stiffer and have less flex than those with thinner walls.

Rigid Cross Country Mountain Bicycle Forks

The geometry of cross country mountain bicycles has changed dramatically since the introduction of the first production frames in the late 1970s. The first suspension forks, which appeared around 1990, only had about 45-50 mm of travel and, as a consequence, had crown-to-axle lengths on par with their rigid counterparts. By 2000, suspension forks with 80 mm of travel were the norm, and the geometry of the mountain bike had to be altered to accommodate a longer fork. At the present date, mass-produced suspension forks with less than 100 mm of travel are very difficult to find. Rigid mountain bicycle forks are still somewhat popular and not rare in the present mass market. Such forks are invariably *suspension corrected* with crown-to-axle lengths on par with suspension forks with 120 mm or more of travel. The fork blades for such rigid forks are very thick with outer diameters as large as 31.8 mm.

When built into a fork with a long crown-to-axle length (>430 mm), the fork blades typically used in lugged fork construction are too narrow and supple to withstand harsh off-road use. For lighter cross country single track, lugged fork construction might work adequately in terms of function and safety if the builder follows a few guidelines:

1. The crown-to-axle length is 420 mm or shorter.
2. The crown has at least 60 mm of tire clearance.
3. The builder uses bosses for cantilever or V-brakes.
4. The builder does not use a disc tab.
5. The builder cuts from the small ends of the fork blades (if a cut is necessary).
6. Fork rake is between 25 and 45 mm.

Forks built within these guidelines would work better for older mountain bike frames, built around or before 2000. If placed on modern cross country frames, the resulting bicycle would likely have a very low bottom bracket, a steep head angle, and suffer from very twitchy steering.

In the realm of mountain biking, head angle is used as a proxy for fork trail to predict steering quality. Part of the reason for this surrogate is that trail changes as the fork compresses. Regardless, the builder of a cross country mountain bike fork can use the equations in the next chapter to predict bicycle handling. Desirable trail is around 70 mm, with a head angle between 69 and 71 degrees.

Over Locknut Dimension

Over locknut dimension (OLD) is the distance between the outer surfaces of the two locknuts of a wheel hub. The distance between the inner surfaces of the two dropouts of a fork must correspond to the front wheel's OLD. For most modern front bicycle wheel hubs, OLD is 100mm.

Chapter 5: Quantitative Bicycle Fork Design (Optional)

In the previous chapter, I provide a table (Table 4-1) for estimating target crown-to-axle length and rake based on the various bicycle classifications (road bicycle, cyclocross, etc.). Though data from this table can be used to build a fork with appropriate handling characteristics within a given class of cycling discipline, when used alone these data do not allow the builder to fine tune a fork and frame combination to obtain a specific desired head angle, tope tube slope, or fork trail. Quantitative fork design uses trigonometric calculations to enhance fork-building precision. The methods presented in this chapter are completely optional. Those with math phobias may wish to skip this chapter completely.

Data Management Software

Performing the calculations required for quantitative fork design using pencil, paper and calculator is extremely cumbersome and will inevitably result in errors. The use of data management spreadsheets, such as Microsoft Excel or iWork, greatly facilitates quantitative design. Once the builder has built and debugged a fork design spreadsheet, he can easily tweak a fork design by making small changes to the frame and fork input parameters until his output is consistent with a desired and feasible build. Likewise, the builder can use the same spreadsheet over and over again, entering different data for completely different builds.

A comprehensive tutorial about data management spreadsheets is beyond the scope of this text. I will, however, provide the reader with a few pointers and attempt to use notation standard to most spreadsheet software packages.

You should organize and classify your input and output variables and data to minimize confusion. I recommend placing input variables and data, such as frame angles and fork rake, on the left of the spreadsheet. Final output variables, such as trail, bottom bracket drop, and head angle, should go in the middle. Intermediate steps required for output calculations should go on the right.

The following abbreviations apply to most spreadsheet software packages:

"sin" means "sine"

"cos" means "cosine"

"tan" means "tangent"

"asin" means "arcsine"

"acos" means "arccosine"

"atan" means "arctangent"

"/" means "divided by," so "2/2" means "2 divided by 2"

"*" means "multiplied by" or "times," so "2*2" means "2 times 2"

"sqrt" means "square root," so "sqrt(4)" would mean "square root of 4"

"^" means "raised to the power of," so "2^2" would mean "2 raised to the power of

 2" or "2 squared"

You should use code or syntax that is item (variable) based rather than typing numbers into calculation equations. For example, if you know a wheel's diameter is 680 mm but wanted to calculate the radius, you should not simply type "= 680/2." Rather, you should label a cell (data entry square) as "wheel diameter" and place the value in the adjacent cell. (We will pretend this cell has coordinates B12). You could label another cell as "wheel radius" and code the adjacent cell as "= B12/2" which asks the computer to divide the number in B12 by 2 and display the answer. With this construct, you can change the wheel diameter (by simply changing the number in cell B12) and obtain instantaneous results for all other affected dependent parameters. Of course, code and syntax will be specific to whatever spreadsheet program you use.

You need to be aware of your spreadsheet's default settings for angles. For example, the spreadsheet may assume that you always enter angles as radians instead of degrees and want your angles outputted as radians. (This schematic is the default for Microsoft Excel). If radians are the default setting, you would have to tell the computer to convert input angles in degrees to radians and output angles from radians to degrees. For example, typing in something like "= sin(radians(a))" would mean "take my angle 'a' in degrees and convert my angle to radians and then give me the sine of this angle." Likewise, when calculating an angle, you may have to type something like "= degrees(atan(A/B))" which would mean "take length of A divided by B, find me the angle that has this ratio as a tangent, and convert this angle from radians to degrees."

Basic Trigonometry

For the remainder of the chapter, I will present equations as if they were syntax entered into a Microsoft Excel spreadsheet. Although this will facilitate syntax coding and data management, the equations will appear rather cluttered in this text. If the reader has difficulty understanding the math, he may wish to rewrite the equations on a separate piece of paper, leaving out the words "radians" and "degrees" and the extra parentheses that accompany these functions.

The reader must understand basic trigonometry to properly design a frame using quantitative methods. For those readers who spent high school math class daydreaming about cheerleaders (or football players), I provide a review of trigonometric functions below. (The author was so unpopular in high school among cheerleaders that he did not even bother to dream. Undistracted, he went on to pursue a degree in statistics).

For any triangle, the angle measurements of all three angles must add up to 180 degrees. A right triangle is a triangle in which one of the three angles is a right angle or measures 90 degrees (Figure 5-1).

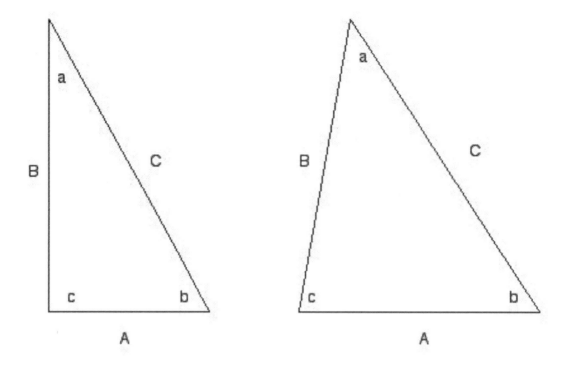

Figure 5-1: *Lower case letters refer to angles and uppercase letters refer to the lengths of sides. The triangle on the left is a right triangle because angle c measures 90 degrees. The triangle on the right is not a right triangle because neither angle a, b, nor c measures 90 degrees.*

For a right triangle, the shorter length sides are called *legs* and the longest side, which is always opposite the right angle, is called the *hypotenuse*. For the right triangle in Figure 5-1 above, in which C is the hypotenuse, the following formula is the Pythagorean theorem:

C^2 = A^2 + B^2

For a right triangle, trigonometric functions useful to calculate unknown side lengths include:

sin(a) = A/C (opposite leg length divided by hypotenuse)

cos(a) = B/C (adjacent leg divided by hypotenuse)

tan(a) = A/B (opposite leg divided by adjacent leg)

For a right triangle, trigonometric functions useful to calculate unknown angles include:

a = asin(A/C)

a = acos(B/C)

a = atan(A/B)

For non-right triangles, the following formulas are extremely useful to calculate unknown angles and/or side lengths:

Law of cosines: $C^2 = A^2 + B^2 - 2*A*B*cos(c)$

Law of sines: $sin(a)/A = sin(b)/B = sin(c)/C$

Of course, before you make any calculation, you must make sure the available known data describe one and only one triangle. The following data describe a unique triangle and will allow you to calculate all unknown sides and/or angles: three sides (SSS); one side and the adjacent angles (ASA); one angle and the adjacent sides (SAS).

The following data describe more than one possible triangle and will not allow you to calculate unknown sides and/or angles: three angles but no sides (AAA); a side and two angles but one angle is not adjacent to the side (AAS); an angle and two sides but one side is not adjacent to the angle (SSA or ASS in the vernacular dialect).

Measuring Tubes

For the purposes of this chapter, tube lengths of a bicycle frame are measured center-to-center (c-c), meaning that a tube is measured from the center of the intersections of the long axes of adjacent tubes. Part of the measurement may lie entirely off of the tube in question. For example, a seat tube is measured from the center of the bottom bracket, where the bottom bracket spindle would lie, to the middle of the intersection of the top tube.

Quantitative Fork Design Model Assumptions

Some bicycle design purists draw life size diagrams of their frames and forks that incorporate such variables as tube width. Others use fancy computer-aided design (CAD) programs to handle every single detail and display scale drawings. The approach used in this chapter simplifies the frame to prevent calculations from becoming unnecessarily cumbersome.

Our conceptual model projects the three dimensional bicycle frame and fork combination into a single plane. An appropriate metaphor would be to imagine that we held the frame over a level surface with the sun directly overhead (solar noon). Our model would be the shadow of the frame, with the two rear triangles superimposed on one-another as a single triangle. The shadows of the stay lengths would be shorter than the actual stay lengths. We further simplify our model by eliminating all tube widths, thinning them down to infinity thin line segments that connect with one another center-to-center. If our fork has bent blades, they magically straighten out and become offset at an angle relative to the steering axis that preserves the location of the front dropouts, the length of the rake, and the crown-to-axle distance. A drawing of our model would look very similar to Figure 2-1 (Chapter 2). Our model provides angle and center-to-center length estimates with very good precision (but is not 100% accurate).

Example Fork

Most students learn mathematical concepts much easier when the teacher walks them through concrete examples. Only a weird few possess the ability to internalize concepts by simply reading annoyingly long proofs spelled out in math jargon.

In the example that follows, we assume the bicycle frame is already constructed. We already know tube and stay lengths and frame angles. Furthermore, these parameters are fixed and cannot be changed. The hypothetical problem we wish to solve is what will be the resulting seat tube angle, head angle, fork trail, bottom bracket height, top tube slope, wheelbase, and front center for a given fork rake and crown-to-axle length. The idea is that, to design our fork, we plug and chug different fork rakes and crown-to-axle lengths until we achieve desirable outcome values (head angle, trail, etc.). Note that the equations below are valid even if we wanted to design the fork and frame together (meaning our frame parameters would not be fixed).

Our example frame and fork is the following:

A builder already has a road bicycle frame that fits him well. The chain stays (CS) and down tube (DT) lengths (measured center-to-center) are 435 mm and 618 mm long, respectively. The frame has the following angles: CS-CS of 7 degrees; CS-ST of 61 degrees; ST-DT of 60 degrees; DT-HT of 120 degrees; ST-TT of 73 degrees. He intends to use 700c wheels with 28 mm tires. He wants to know how placing a fork with a rake and crown-to-axle length of 45 mm and 380 mm, respectively, will affect seat tube angle, head angle, fork trail, bottom bracket height, top tube slope, wheelbase, and front center.

Note that other frame measurements, specifically seat tube (ST) and top tube (TT) lengths, are the usual starting points in frame design. However, because we are designing a fork, these parameters are not necessary to solve the problem at hand provided we know the other parameters listed above.

<u>Projecting the Chain Stays into the Model</u>

Before we can proceed, we need to adjust our actual measurements so that they comply with our conceptual (and mathematical) modeling technique. Our builder has 435 mm chain stays, but they point outward at 7 degree angles (CS-CS angle) relative to the plane of our front triangle. Our model requires a completely two-dimensional structure, so we need to project our chain stays into the same plane as the front triangle. This projection will effectively shorten our chain stays but preserves the horizontal and vertical locations of our dropouts (meaning they will not move forwards, backwards, up, or down relative the bottom bracket shell). To find the new length of our projected chain stays, we can look at Figure 5-1 (left) and pretend our bottom bracket shell is at the top of the triangle. The side C would, therefore, be the chain stay; the angle 'a' would be the CS-CS angle; and B would be the adjusted chain stay length projected into the plane of the front triangle. We can apply some algebra to the formula for cosine:

$$B = \cos(\text{radians}(a))*C = \cos(\text{radians}(7))* 435 \text{ mm} = 432 \text{ mm}.$$

Clearly, this adjustment is nearly negligible. Indeed, we could skip this adjustment all together and still arrive at reasonably accurate estimates of bottom bracket drop, head angle, etc.

<u>Incorporating the Fork into the Model</u>

Unfortunately, our data require an additional set of adjustments to comply with our mathematical modeling technique. In reality, the fork crown is not located at the c-c intersection of the down tube and head tube (as in Figure 2-1, Chapter 2). Rather, the crown is located below this distance, at the end of the head tube and lower headset cup. To correct the model, we draw in an additional set of lines: a connection between the front dropouts and the c-c DT-HT intersection; the steering axis; the rake (which connects our dropouts to the steering axis at a right angle); a short downward extension of the head tube; and a connection between the head tube extension and the dropouts, our crown-to-axle length (Figure 5-2).

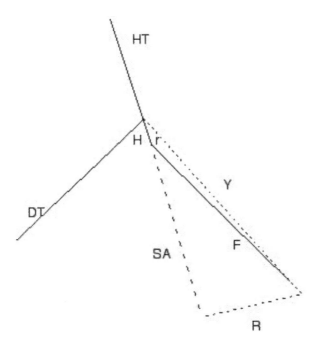

Figure 5-2: *Model Corrections. Capital letters refer to the lengths of sides. Lowercase letters refer to angles. Dashed lines are imaginary lines. H is the distance from the top of the fork crown to the c-c HT-DT intersection; F is the crown-to-axle length of the fork; R is the rake (offset) of the fork; SA is the length of the steering axis and lies along the same line as H; Y is the adjusted "model" fork length; r is the angle between SA and Y. By definition of rake, the angle between SA and R is 90 degrees.*

To estimate H, we send our hypothetical builder to measures the distance between the c-c HT-DT intersection to the top of the fork crown (below the headset) of another lugged bicycle he keeps in his garage. He finds that H is 40 mm.

Using the Pythagorean theorem and some algebra:

SA = sqrt(F^2 – R^2) = sqrt (380 mm^2 – 40 mm^2) = 377 mm.

Looking at Figure 5-2, we realize that Y is the hypotenuse of a right triangle with one leg R and the other leg the sum of SA and H. Using the Pythagorean theorem:

Y = sqrt(R^2 + (H + SA)^2) = sqrt(45 mm^2 + (40 mm + 377 mm)^2) = 420 mm.

Lastly, we calculate the angle r:

r = degrees(asin(R/Y)) = degrees(asin(45 mm/420 mm)) = 6.2 degrees.

Calculating Bottom Bracket Drop, Bottom Bracket Height, Wheelbase, and Front Center

We continue to draw our model, incorporating the new adjusted fork and adjusted chain stays. To simplify our drawing, we can omit the seat stays, seat tube, and top tube (Figure 5-3) because these measurements are not yet required. We assume the rider will use the same size tires and rims on the front and rear wheels, which means both the front and rear dropouts are the same distance from the ground. We draw three imaginary lines: One line connects the bottom bracket to the front dropouts, which is front center; one line connects the rear dropouts to the front dropouts, which would be parallel to the ground and measure the wheelbase; and a third line, perpendicular to the ground, connects the bottom bracket to the wheelbase line. This last line has the same measurement as the bottom bracket drop.

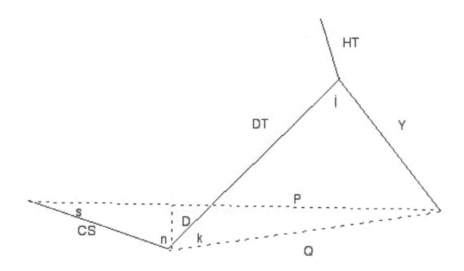

Figure 5-3: *HT = head tube; DT = down tube; CS= adjusted chain stay; Y = adjusted fork length; D = bottom bracket drop; Q = front center; P = wheelbase; j = the sum of the supplement to the HT-DT angle and r from our previous set of calculations; k = angle between D and Q; n = DT-CS angle (sum of DT-ST and ST-CS angle); s = angle between CS and P.*

We calculate j, the angle between Y and DT, as 180 minus (the supplement to) the HT-DT angle plus r (from Figure 5-2):

j = (180 – 120) + 6.2 = 66.2 degrees.

Using the law of cosines and some algebra, we get Q, front center:

Q = sqrt(DT^2 + Y^2 – 2*DT*Y*cos(radians(j)))

Q = sqrt(618 mm^2 + 420 mm^2 – 2*618 mm*420 mm*cos(radians(66.2 degrees)))

Q = 591mm.

The law of sines and some algebra gives us angle k:

k = degrees(asin(sin(radians(j))*Y/Q))

k = degrees(asin(sin(radians(66.2 degrees))*420 mm/591 mm)) = 40.6 degrees.

Before we find P, we must determine the angle between the CS and Q. We call this angle "m". Note that m is omitted from Figure 5-3 to prevent the figure from becoming too cluttered, and m is simply the sum of n and k:

 m = n + k = 121 degrees + 40.6 degrees = 161.6 degrees.

We get P from the law of cosines and algebra:

P = sqrt(Q^2 + CS^2 – 2*Q*CS*cos(radians(m)))

P = sqrt(591 mm^2 + 432 mm^2 – 2*591 mm*432 mm*cos(radians(161.6 degrees)))

P = 1009 mm, the wheelbase of the frame.

To get D, we need s, so we use the law of sines and algebra:

s = degrees(asin(sin(radians(m))*Q/P))

s = degrees(asin(sin(radians(161.6 degrees))*591 mm/1009 mm))

s = 10.7 degrees.

Because D is oriented perpendicular to the ground and the dropouts are at the same height, P is parallel to the ground and perpendicular to D. Therefore, the relationship between s, CS and D is simply:

sin(radians(s)) = D/CS, which (with some algebra) gives us D = CS*sin(radians(s))

D = 432mm* sin(radians(10.7 degrees)) = 80 mm, which is the bottom bracket drop.

To calculate bottom bracket height, we need to know the outer diameter of our wheel. We tell our hypothetical builder to place a 28 mm tire on his 700c wheel (ISO 622 mm) and measure the diameter from the outsides of the tire. The outer diameter is 678 mm, and the radius is half of this or 339 mm. Bottom bracket height is simply:

Wheel radius – bottom bracket drop (D)

339 mm – 80 mm = 259 mm.

This bottom bracket height of 259 mm works well for road riding. However, if the rider uses this frame, fork, wheel, and tire combination for single track, he might find downward toe clearance to be problematic, frequently clipping a pedal on rocks and roots.

Toe overlap will be at a maximum when one crank lies along front center, the imaginary line Q. We assume our hypothetical builder will equip the bicycle with 170mm cranks. Toe overlap can be estimated as follows:

Toe overlap = Q – crank length – wheel radius

Toe overlap = 591 mm – 170 mm – 339 mm = 82 mm.

Forward toe clearance of 82 mm is tight. If the rider wears big shoes, his toes may touch the tire if he makes wide, low speed turns.

Calculating Head Angle, Seat Angle, Top Tube Incline, and Fork Trail

To calculate seat angle, we modify our model drawing. We ignore everything in front of the bottom bracket, and draw a straight line through the bottom bracket parallel to the imaginary line P that connects the front and rear dropouts. This line is, therefore, parallel to the ground (Figure 5-4). We also draw in our seat tube.

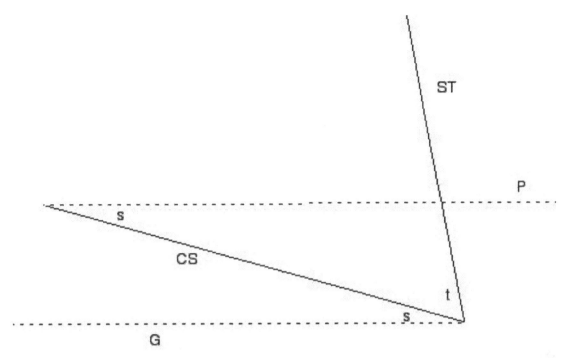

Figure 5-4: The lines *P and G run parallel to the ground and are parallel to one another. ST = Seat tube; CS = adjusted chain stay; t = the ST-CS angle; s = angle between the CS and P, (which has the same measurement as the angle between CS and G).*

The reader may recall, from high school geometry, the transversal postulate. The transversal postulate dictates that, because P and G are parallel lines, s (the angle between CS and P) will have the same measurement as the angle between CS and G. The seat angle is, therefore, simply the sum of s and t (the ST-CS angle):

seat angle = s + t = 10.7 + 61 = 71.7 degrees.

We determine head angle as follows:

head angle = seat angle – (DT-ST angle + (DT-HT angle – 180 degrees))

head angle = 71.7 degrees – (60 degrees + (120 degrees – 180 degrees)) = 71.7 degrees.

We calculate top tube incline in a similar fashion as head angle:

TT incline = ST-TT angle - seat angle

TT incline = 73 degrees – 71.7 degrees = 1.3 degrees.

Moving toward the front of the bicycle, the top tube will rise 1.3 degrees relative to the ground. To all but the most astute observer, the top tube will appear to be parallel to the ground.

Finally, we can calculate fork trail using the formula from Chapter 4:

Fork trail = (wheel radius*cos(radians(head angle)) - rake)/sin(radians(head angle))

Fork trail = (339 mm*cos(radians(71.7 degrees))- 45 mm)/sin(radians(71.7 degrees))

Fork trail = 65 mm.

Let us pretend our hypothetical builder is dissatisfied with these results, wanting a top tube perfectly parallel to the ground and a fork trail of 55 mm. Because we already have our spreadsheet set up, the extra calculations are hardly burdensome. The measurements of our hypothetical frame are fixed and cannot be changed, so the only parameters we can alter are fork rake and crown-to-axle length. We can simply plug and chug different numbers for rake and crown-to-axle length, throwing out results we do not like. If, for example, we enter a crown-to-axle length of 362 mm and rake of 48 mm, our top tube incline becomes 0.3 degrees and trail 55.2 mm, results much closer to the builder's target values.

Other Calculations

The example calculations above were selected primarily to demonstrate how to use trigonometric functions, the law of sines, and the law of cosines to design a fork. The reader does not necessarily need to use the same approach as the example. For example, he could start with known seat tube and top tube lengths but an unknown down tube. Alternatively, rather than designing a fork with frame parameters fixed, he could design the frame and fork simultaneously, altering both frame and fork parameters until he arrives at desirable results. As long as the reader can conceptualize a frame based on polygons that can be subdivided into triangles, the calculations are straightforward and follow the general premise as the sample calculations above.

Downloading Data Management Spreadsheet for Free

The webpage http://luggedbicycle.weebly.com/technical-support.html contains a free downloadable copy of a Microsoft Excel spreadsheet. The spreadsheet contains formulae notations and abbreviations nearly identical to those in this chapter. Note, however, that a builder who slogs through the work and the inevitable errors and frustration required to develop his own spreadsheet will learn much more than merely how to plug and chug numbers.

Chapter 6: Recommended Tools

In this chapter, I describe the tools and materials required to shape metal, to measure fork parts, and to construct jigs. Torches are described in the next chapter. The decision to buy high quality tools versus less durable, cheaper tools is an important dilemma for the novice builder. If you only want to build a single fork, or are unsure if you will build more forks (or frames) later on, the purchase of cheaper tools may be a sound financial option. If you know you want to build many forks, high quality tools are necessary because cheap tools tend to wear out. Retailers such as Sears, Lowes, Home Depot, and Ace Hardware stock quality tools. Affordable tools are available at Harbor Freight. Harbor Freight's house brands Chicago Electric and Chicago Welding function well and are surprisingly durable.

Bench Vise

A vise is mandatory (Figure 6-1). The vise secures fork parts, freeing up both of the builder's hands to work, shape, or measure. Attempting to secure a metal part with one hand while trying to cut, file, grind, or drill with the other is an imprecise and inefficient methodology. The vise should have jaws that open up to at least 50 mm (2"). You must bolt down your vise securely to a sturdy workbench or table. (An old door or piece of plywood nailed to two saw horses works adequately well as a fork or frame building workstation).

(The reader might notice that the vise that appears in the photos of Chapters 9 onward is not bolted down. While shooting photos, I left one vise free to allow me to quickly pick and choose the location with the best light quality. The purpose of the photos is to demonstrate a layout that allows the builder to perform certain tasks efficiently and effectively. The photos were shot in a static state where neither hands, nor tools, nor fork parts were moving. The actual work described by these photos involved dynamic states requiring a different vise bolted to a work table. Unfortunately, the actual work vise [Figure 6-1] was in a location with poor light quality).

You should prepare your vise so that the hard steel jaws are less likely to crimp, scratch, or dent the lugs or tubes. You will need epoxy glue and a strip of aluminum angle purchased at a hardware store or metal fabrication shop. The width of each angle on the strip should be slightly bigger than the height of the gripping surfaces of the vise jaws. With a hacksaw, you should cut off two strips from the aluminum angle. Each strip should be slightly longer than the width of the vise jaws. File the cut ends of the strips smooth, removing all burrs. Mix your epoxy, and apply a thin layer to the vise jaws and the insides of the two aluminum angle strips. Place the strips of aluminum angle on each vise jaw so that the insides of the angles cover the gripping surfaces and tops of the vise jaws (Figure 6-1). Close the jaws slowly, ensuring the aluminum angles do not slip. You should torque down the handle so that the aluminum strips are clamped against each other tightly. Allow fifteen hours for the epoxy to cure. When the aluminum strips become worn, remove them with a hammer and punch and apply new ones.

Figure 6-1: *The author's working bench vise. Note that the vise has been bolted securely to the work bench and that aluminum angles have been glued to the vise jaws to minimize the risk of scratching and denting fork parts.*

Hacksaw

A hacksaw is mandatory (Figure 6-2). In the procedures that follow in Chapters 9 onward, any step that requires a cut from a hacksaw implies that the part in question must be secured in the jaws of a vise. When using a hacksaw, use long strokes to cut with the entire length of the blade and not just the middle.

Half Round File

A half round file is mandatory (Figure 6-2). In the procedures that follow in Chapters 9 onward, any step that requires filing implies that the part in question must be secured in the jaws of a vise. The flat surface of the file is useful to square off the ends of fork blades after (imperfect) hacksaw cuts, to file flat metal surfaces, or to file down burrs or globs of brazing alloy flush with adjacent metallic contours. The round surface of the file is useful to file curves or irregular contours. After brazing, the very edges of the file can be used to file excess brazing alloy from the shoreline of a lugged joint.

The best way to use a file is to hold the handle with your dominant hand and place downward pressure near the front of the file with your non-dominant hand. File as you push forward and not as you pull back during recovery.

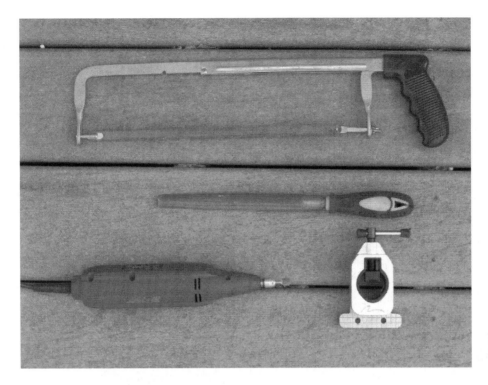

Figure 6-2: *Tools that assist the shaping of metal. From top to bottom, left to right: hacksaw, half round file, rotary tool, steering tube cutting guide.*

Rotary Tool

A rotary tool (Figure 6-2) is necessary to grind or clean the inner surfaces of sockets and fork blades. The half round file will not fit into tight spaces. A drill equipped with a grinding stone is not an adequate substitute for a rotary tool. In the procedures that follow in Chapters 9 onward, any step that requires grinding, sanding, or shaping with a rotary tool implies that the part in question must be secured in the jaws of a vise.

Generic rotary tool handles generally work as well as brand name handles. However, I find brand name rotary tool bits, such as Dremel, to be superior to generic bits. You will require one small (1/4" [6.35mm]) aluminum oxide grinding stone and one very small diamond burr bit. A small (1/4" [6.35mm]) drum sanding mandrel with 120 grit or coarser bands is optional. When set to low revolutions, a grinding stone functions adequately as a sanding mandrel. You need the grinding stone (at high revolutions) to enlarge the openings of fork crown and dropout sockets when the fit is too tight. Before brazing, you can use the sanding mandrel (or grinding bit set to low revolution speed) to clean the inner contours of sockets or fork blades until the metal shines. When sanding, do not apply too much downward pressure or you will remove too much metal, causing parts to fit loosely. A strip of emery cloth or sand paper wrapped around a narrow tube or finger also works to clean the inner surfaces of sockets.

Steering Tube Cutting Guide (Optional)

Though not required, a steering tube cutting guide enables precise hacksaw cuts (Figures 6-2 and 6-3). The steering tube cutting guide has three components: a clamp that secures the guide to the tube to be cut; a slot to guide the hacksaw blade; and a tab that allows the guide to be secured in a vise. The builder can use the guide to cut the steering tube and the large ends of the fork blades. The small ends of the fork blades are too small to fit in the guide properly, unless a strip of metal (such as a worn flat file) is placed underneath the tube and within the guide.

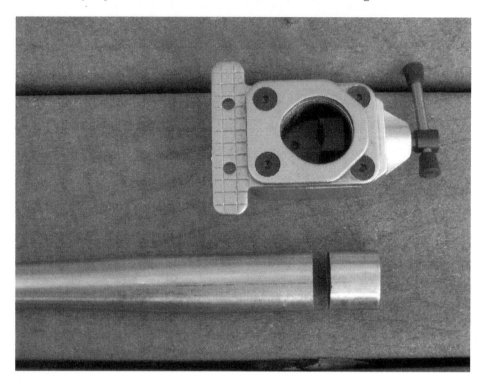

Figure 6-3: *A steering tube cutting guide (top) can help the builder produce precise, square cuts in steering tubes and at the ends of the fork blades (bottom).*

Homemade Tube Bending Mandrel

A tube bending mandrel is necessary to create rake in fork blades unless the builder chooses to build a straight bladed fork or buys pre-bent fork blades (Chapter 3). Professional grade fork blade benders are excellent tools capable of making excellent bends. Unfortunately, such equipment typically costs hundreds of dollars. Amateur builders with limited financial resources can bend fork blades using a combination of ice and a homemade tube bending mandrel.

To construct a tube bending mandrel, acquire a board of hardwood, such as oak, that measures at least 2' (61 cm) long, 7.5" (19 cm) wide, and ¾" (19 mm) thick. Softwoods such as pine are inadequate and will break, dent, or otherwise deform under load. Cut the board of hardwood across its width into two equal lengths. Locate a large circular object with a diameter between 355 and 455 mm. (The rotating platter of a large microwave usually meets this criteria). Place one of the hardwood boards on a level surface. Place the circular object over the board so that the contours of the circle lie tangent to the lower left hand corner and the top of the board (Figure 6-4). Trace the contours of the circle onto the board with a pencil (Figure 6-4). Repeat drawing the guideline with the other board. Using a handheld jig saw or coping saw, cut along the guidelines of both boards (Figure 6-5). Err on the side of cutting outside the guideline rather than inside.

Figure 6-4: *To prepare a homemade tube bending mandrel, trace the contours of a large circular object onto a board of hardwood.*

Figure 6-5: *To prepare a homemade tube bending mandrel, use a jig saw or coping saw to cut along the circular guideline.*

To create a V-shaped notch along the top of the mandrel, use a rasp, file, or sander to shape a bevel along the circular contours of the two boards (Figure 6-6). Try to angle the bevel as close as possible to forty five degrees. The bevels of the two hardwood boards need to be mirror images of one another to create the V-shape (Figures 6-7 and 6-8).

Figure 6-6: *To prepare a homemade tube bending mandrel, create a forty-five degree angled bevel along the circular contours of the hardwood boards. In this figure, the builder uses an angle grinder with a sanding wheel to perform this task. A rasp also works effectively.*

Place the two boards together, so that the rectangular contours of the boards align with one another. Mark with a pencil where the inner contours of the bevels do not align (Figure 6-7). Reshape the wood at these marks with a file or rasp until the inner contours of the bevels of the two boards align well with one another.

Apply wood glue to the inner surfaces of the two boards and clamp them together so that the inner contours of the beveled edges align with one another. Allow the glue to dry overnight. At this point onward, we will refer to the wooden, curved, notched structure as the *mandrel body*.

Drill two holes approximately 6 mm in dimeter approximately 25mm from the bottom of the mandrel body. One hole should lie approximately 40 mm from the front, roundest edge of the mandrel and the other should lie approximately 40 mm from the rear, less round edge. Acquire two pieces of aluminum angle measuring approximately 5 mm in thickness, 50 mm in width and 60 to 100 cm in length. Place the wooden mandrel body over one of the aluminum angles so that the bottom of the wood lies flush with the bottom of the angle. Only 10 to 15 cm of aluminum angle should protrude beyond the front round contour of the wooden mandrel body (Figure 6-8). Much of the angle should protrude beyond the back of the wooden mandrel body (Figure 12-2, Chapter 12). Use the holes in the wood as guides to drill through the angle. Repeat this process to drill holes in the remaining angle.

Figure 6-7: *Using a pencil to mark where the inner contours of the bevels do not align.*

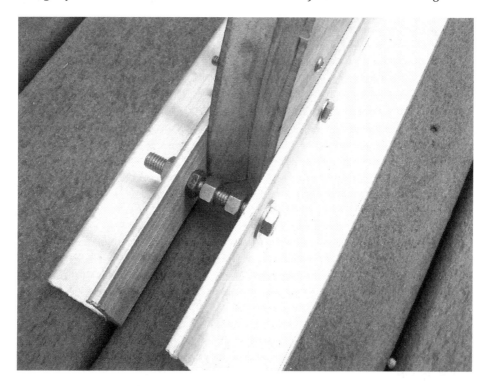

Figure 6-8: *The dropout rest (bolt) lies as close as possible to the front of the wooden mandrel.*

Use long two long 6 mm bolts, two 6mm nuts, and four washers to bolt the mandrel body and two aluminum angles together (Figure 6-8). Trace the round contours of the front of the mandrel body onto the inside of both of the aluminum angles. Transfer the mark at the top inner surfaces of the angles onto the top widths of the angles. Disassemble the mandrel assembly. Drill a 9 mm or 3/8" hole through one of the aluminum angles. This hole represents the location of the dropout rest. The hole should occur midway up the width of the angle and should occur as close as possible to the guideline mark that represents the front of the wooden mandrel body. No part of the hole should extend through the guideline. Moving the hole further away from the front of the mandrel will create fork blade bends farther up the fork blade and farther away from the dropouts. Bends closer to the dropouts appear more elegant than those farther away. Place the two aluminum angles next to each other so that the bottoms lie flush with one another and the marks at the top widths (that represent the front contours of the wooden mandrel) align. Clamp the angles together and use the 9 mm or 3/8" hole in the drilled angle as a guide to drill a hole in the remaining angle. Reassemble the mandrel assembly and place a 9 mm or 3/8" bolt through the holes in front of the mandrel assembly. Use washers and 9 mm or 3/8" nuts to secure the bolt in place (Figure 6-8). The thick bolt will secure the dropout when the builder bends the fork blades (Figure 12-2, Chapter 12).

To achieve leverage during bending, you will need to acquire a tube approximately 5' (150 cm) long. An aluminum tube with a 1 ¼" x 1 ¼"" (32 mm x 32 mm) square cross section and 1/8" (3 mm) thick walls fits well over the large oval end of fork blades. The long axis of the oval fits into the diagonal of the inner contour of the square cross section (Figure 12-2, Chapter 12).

(Of all the photos of bent blades in this text, only those portrayed in Figures 14-1 and 14-7 [Chapter 14] were created with the mandrel assembly described above. The bent blades portrayed in other photos were created using an inferior method and are, therefore, less elegant.)

Metric Measuring Tape

The procedures in this manual require accurate measurements of linear distance. A metric measuring tape (Figure 6-9) allows accurate measurements to the nearest millimeter. The measuring tape need not be longer than one meter. The imperial scale requires the builder to change denominators between each mark on his tape, which can create confusion and inaccuracy. When using a measuring tape, the frame part need not be secured in a vise under most circumstances.

Calipers (Optional)

Metric calipers (Figure 6-9) allow linear measurement of outer or inner diameters of tubes, plugs, or sockets to the nearest 0.1 mm. If you are using socketed dropouts, calipers are usually not necessary to build a fork. However, if you are using plugged dropouts and the dropouts are not a drop-in fit, calipers may serve as a guide to reshape your plugs, to find the locations along the fork blades' tapers where the plugs might fit, or to predict gap size prior to brazing (Chapters 8 and 12).

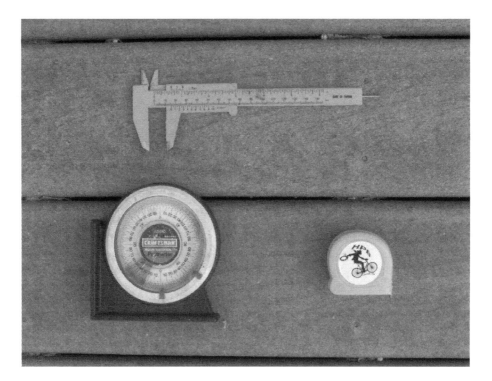

Figure 6-9: *Measuring tools, from top to bottom, left to right: calipers, inclinometer, metric tape measure.*

Inclinometer

An inclinometer (Figure 6-9) is a device that allows us to determine an object's angle relative to gravity. Some manufacturers also call this device a protractor. In this manual, an inclinometer is necessary to align our fork properly. We will use an inclinometer to help us orient an object either *perpendicular to the ground*, meaning the measured surface should be vertical, or *parallel to the ground*, meaning the measured surface should be horizontal. The inclinometer must be used in conjunction with a vise that is securely bolted to a work bench or table.

When using an inclinometer, the general procedure is as follows: clamp the fork part loosely in the vise; place the inclinometer along the side or top surface of the part; move the object within the vise (while securing the inclinometer with your hand) until the inclinometer displays a reading of either 0 or 90 degrees; and then tighten down the vise jaws so the fork part cannot move.

Drill

An electric drill (Figure 15-1, Chapter 15) is necessary to drill hot gas vent holes required during brazing and to drill the caliper brake mounting holes through the crown and steering tube. Even if the builder does not want to use caliper brakes, a hole through the crown and steering tube is useful to mount fenders or other bicycle parts. A standard 3/8" (9.5 mm) hand drill works well. Drills with keyless chucks do not secure bits as tightly as drills with keyed chucks. A variable speed drill that allows a low revolution speed is better for drilling through steel. In the procedures that follow in Chapters 9 onward, any step that requires drilling implies that the part in question must be secured in the jaws of a vise.

Titanium nitride bits work well when drilling through metal. The builder will require 3 mm, 4 mm, 5 mm, and 6 mm bits. An 8 mm bit is required in some circumstances (discussed below). To enhance precision and to avoid premature wear of your bits, a good procedure is to drill a small hole and re-drill with progressively larger bits until you create the appropriately sized hole. If metric drill bits are not available, 1/8", 3/16", and ¼" bits work marginally well in place of 3 mm, 5 mm, and 6 mm bits respectively.

When drilling through steel, you should use a slow drill speed. Drops of cutting oil applied to the steel surface and drill bit will expedite drilling and preserve the service life of the bit.

Drilling through a metallic surface can be tricky because the bit will have a tendency to roll out of place before it bites into the metal. Outwardly curved surfaces such as tubes are particularly problematic. A small dimple can help with such surfaces. Mark the location of the surface where you want to drill, place the point of a center punch on the mark, and tap the punch firmly with a hammer. A single blow should place a small dimple into the surface. The dimple will help the bit bite through the surface.

Hand Reamer (Optional)

A hand reamer (Figure 15-2, Chapter 15) is useful to de-burr drill holes. Some brake calipers require an 8 mm hole in the back of the fork crown and steering tube. A hand reamer can bore out a 6 mm (or ¼") hole to 8 mm if an 8mm drill bit is unavailable.

Jigging Materials

Jigs (also known as fixtures) help to preserve a fork's alignment during the brazing process. The builder will require a 3/8" (9.5 mm) threaded rod at least 150 mm (6") in length with six nuts to jig the dropouts in place (Figures 11-3 and 11-4, Chapter 11). If available, a 9 mm bolt and 9 mm nuts fit front dropouts better than a 3/8" rod. Two adjustable wrenches are necessary to tighten down and lock the nuts in place.

A front wheel (Figure 13-7, Chapter 13) or the threaded rod (Figures 14-4 and 14-5, Chapter 14) can work as a fixture to braze the fork blades into the fork crown. A front rack block with a quick release skewer, such as the *Hollywood Rack T970 Fork Block*, allows more rapid jig assembly and disassembly than a threaded rod (Figure 14-1, Chapter 14).

Tube Blocks (Optional)

A tube block can secure the steering tube in the vise during several steps of the fabrication process (Figure 15-1, Chapter 15). The steering tube has a thick wall and, therefore, does not deform easily when clamped directly into a vise. For this reason, tube blocks are not really necessary for lugged fork construction. Tube blocks are available from Paragon Machine Works (refer to references section for web address). If purchased, the inner diameter of the tube block should match the outer diameter of the steering tube. If you plan on building many forks, some with 25.4 mm steerers and others with 28.6 mm, you can save some money by buying a single 28.6 mm tube block and a 28.6 mm to 25.4 mm adaptor (shim) instead of buying blocks of two different sizes (Figure 6-10).

Previous versions of this manual described construction of a jug using tube blocks, a fork block, and aluminum angles. Setting up this jig is cumbersome and enhanced precision only marginally better than using a fork block alone.

Figure 6-10: *A 2" (50.8 mm) square tube block (left) with 28.6 mm bore from Paragon Machine Works. The shim (right) converts the block to a 25.4 mm bore.*

Crown Race Cutting Tool (Optional)

The crown race cutting tool mills down the crown race and faces the top of the crown to properly fit the fork into the headset race ring. When purchased new, the buyer receives two parts: the handle and the blade (Figure 6-11). Blades are not adjustable. Individual blades cost 50% to 75% the price of an entire new tool. Professional crown race cutting tools cost around $450. Budget versions retail around $150. Budget versions only have blades at the bottom of the tool and not within the bore. As a consequence, budget cutters lack precision and frequently create crown races narrower than desired. Most shops will cut a crown race for around $15 to $30. I only recommend you buy a budget crown race cutting tool if crown race cutting services are unavailable at your local bike shop. The use of this tool is described in Chapter 16.

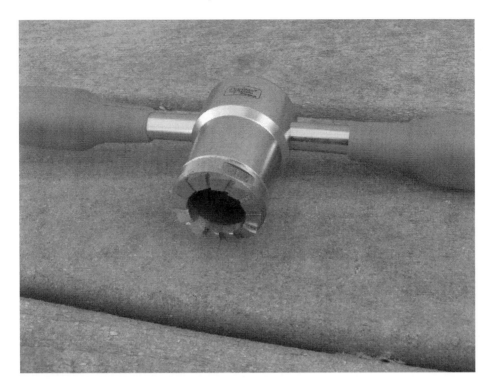

Figure 6-11: *A budget crown race cutting tool with the circular blade (foreground) threaded into the handle (background). Note the absence of blades within the bore of the tool.*

Chapter 7: Torches

The brazing torch is not a magic wand. Although higher quality torches are capable of higher quality brazes, the performance of a torch depends almost entirely on the skill and experience of the builder. A novice builder must learn and understand his torch's operations, capabilities, and limitations.

In this manual's companion publication, *Lugged Bicycle Frame Construction,* I explain that an inexpensive ($40) MAPP-air torch works as an adequate heat source provided the reader picks and chooses frame parts that lie within this torch's limitations. Although I review the use of the MAPP-air torch in this manual, this torch is not sufficient by itself to construct a bicycle fork. The crown and steering tube are too massive for the MAPP-air torch's moderate heat output. An oxy-fuel torch is required to join these two fork parts. An oxy-fuel torch costs several hundred dollars to assemble.

This chapter emphasizes the properties of different oxy-fuels, basic torch operation, and safety. Brazing is covered in the following chapter.

The MAPP-Air Torch

When burnt in air, methylacetylene-propadiene (MAPP) gas produces a flame as hot as 3600F (2000C), which is adequate for silver brazing thin-walled steel structures. This flame is not hot enough for brass brazing, however, which requires an oxy-fuel flame. The MAPP-air torch is also insufficient to bring thick-walled metal pieces to silver brazing temperature. Bicycle parts too thick or massive for MAPP-air silver brazing include the steering tube and the steering tube socket of the fork crown. The MAPP-air torch might be sufficient to braze the fork blade sockets of the crown provided the crown has sloping shoulders and the socket walls are no thicker than 1.3 mm. The MAPP-air torch will work to braze most socketed and plugged dropouts as well as cantilever brake bosses.

The *Bernzomatic MAPP Torch Hose Pressure Regulated Torch Unit* has good ergonomic features, allowing the builder to hook the canister on his belt and effortlessly move the torch with his hand (Figure 7-1). MAPP gas cylinders are cheap ($8 to $10), universally yellow in color, and found in most hardware stores. MAPP gas is much more stable than acetylene and safer to use, store, and transport. Also, compared to the hotter oxy-fuel flame, a MAPP-air flame is less likely to overheat a subassembly brazed by an inexperienced builder. Overheating can distort and weaken metal and exhaust flux. MAPP-air torches produce a broad flame desired for heating the large surface area typical of many lugged joints.

From time to time MAPP gas, which is a proprietary formulation, becomes unavailable in small cylinders in the US. *MAPP-substitute* also comes in yellow canisters and is a blend of propylene (also known as propene) and propane gases. Propylene blends burn slightly cooler than true MAPP gas but work adequately as a substitute in both MAPP-air and oxy-fuel torches.

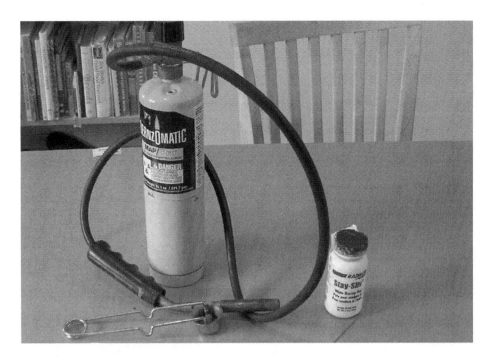

Figure 7-1: *A MAPP-air torch, spark lighter, and silver brazing flux. The MAPP-air torch is insufficient by itself to braze all the joints of a bicycle fork.*

Overview of Oxy-Fuels

The oxy-fuel torch mixes concentrated and pressurized oxygen with a combustible gas to produce a very high temperature flame. The oxy-fuel outfit consists of a compressed oxygen cylinder, a compressed fuel cylinder, a regulator for each cylinder, a double hose, a torch handle, and a welding tip (Figure 7-2). Oxygen and fuel mix within the torch handle.

When mixed with oxygen, propane burns at 2500C (4500F), MAPP burns at 2900C (5300F), and acetylene burns at 3500C (6300F). All of these oxy-fuel flames are sufficient for brass brazing and silver brazing all joints of a steel bicycle frame or fork.

Most frame and fork builders use acetylene as a fuel source. Oxy-acetylene flames are easier to adjust and fine tune compared to other oxy-fuels. However, acetylene is inherently unstable and will ignite without an ignition source if vented at moderate pressures (25 psi/1.7 bar/172kpa). Acetylene is available only at welding specialty stores such as Airgas.

Frame and fork builders often overlook propane, MAPP, and MAPP-substitute as oxy-fuels. These alternative gases will not ignite without an ignition source at moderate pressures and are, therefore, safer to transport, store, and use than acetylene. In small quantities, propane, MAPP, and MAPP-substitute are cheaper than acetylene. Propane, MAPP, and MAPP-substitute are stored under pressure in liquid form in small bottles, which cost $6 to $12 at most hardware stores. An acetylene regulator will not fit on small propane, MAPP, or MAPP-substitute canisters. The *Smith Little Torch Preset Regulator Propane 249-500A* (Figures 7-2 and 7-3) allows the use of propane, MAPP, or MAPP-substitute with standard oxy-acetylene welding outfits in place of acetylene and an acetylene regulator.

Figure 7-2: Left: *an oxy-propane outfit. On top of the propane cylinder is a preset regulator. Right: an inexpensive oxy-fuel torch paired to an oxygen concentrator.*

Inexpensive Oxy-Fuel Outfits

Inexpensive oxy-fuel torches, such as the *Bernzomatic Oxygen MAPP Brazing Kit*, cost as little as sixty dollars and can produce a flame hot enough to braze a fork crown. These torches are designed to work with the small red oxygen canisters available for around ten dollars at many hardware stores. Unfortunately, the physical chemistry of oxygen does not allow safe compression at high pressures in thin-walled canisters. As a consequence, the red canisters only contain a small amount of gas, about one-fortieth the amount of a similarly sized propane or MAPP canister. A red oxygen canister only provides enough oxygen for about twenty minutes of brazing. Unmodified, these torches are not suitable for bicycle frame building. However, a builder can cut off the oxygen regulator and use a barb fitting to connect the torch to an oxygen concentrator (figure 7-2, right). This modification transforms the torch into an adequate fork building tool; however, the manufacturer strongly recommends against the modification of this tool. The Bernzomatic Oxygen MAPP Brazing Kit does not have control knobs on the torch handle, so the flame can only be adjusted with the control knobs on the fuel regulator and oxygen concentrator. We are uncertain if the Bernzomatic Oxygen MAPP Brazing Kit has flashback arrestors, so a builder using this torch should never close the fuel regulator while the oxygen is still flowing; otherwise the flame may reverse direction into the fuel cylinder causing a fire or explosion.

Components of the Industrial Oxy-Fuel Outfit

Oxy-fuel outfits are available from several different manufacturers. The description that follows is generic and does not necessarily pertain to any specific brand. Moreover, this text is intended merely as an overview of the function and operation of the components of the oxy-fuel outfit and is not intended to serve, by itself, as a substitute for an owner's manual or operations guide. For safety purposes, the builder must read the entire operator's manual that accompanies his oxy-fuel outfit. If details in the operator's manual contradict some of the descriptions below, the builder should consider the information in the operator's manual to be more accurate.

Acetylene Cylinder

For improved safety during storage and transportation, acetylene is dissolved in acetone within a binding medium housed in the acetylene cylinder. The smallest acetylene cylinders contain around 10 cubic feet (283L) of gas. A cylinder of this sized contains enough gas to braze an entire fork but not enough for an entire frame. For safety purposes, the cylinder should never be stored upside down or on its side. The valve opens with a cylinder valve wrench, which must be kept near the cylinder at all times. When in use, the valve should be opened counterclockwise only ¾ to 1 ½ turns to allow rapid shut off in the event of an emergency. The acetylene cylinder must never be used without a pressure-reducing regulator. The valve should be closed when the builder finishes brazing. Filling a 10 cubic feet acetylene cylinder using the exchange system costs on average $20 to $30.

An acetylene cylinder should not be emptied to an intra-cylinder pressure below 25 psi (1.7 bar/172kpa). Low pressures can dislodge or damage the binding medium housed within the cylinder.

Oxygen Cylinder

Oxygen cylinders with thick steel walls (Figure 7-2, left) can safely contain oxygen compressed to 3,000psi (206bar/20,600kpa). The smallest steel oxygen cylinders contain 20 cubic feet (566L) of oxygen, which is sufficient to build a fork and an entire frame. When in use, the oxygen cylinder valve should be opened completely by turning counterclockwise. Oxygen sold from welding supply stores contains impurities and should not be inhaled directly. Filling a 20 cubic foot oxygen cylinder costs on average $15 to $30. The oxygen cylinder must never be used without a pressure-reducing regulator. The valve should be closed when the builder finishes brazing.

Acetylene Regulator

The purpose of the acetylene regulator (Figure 7-3) is to receive high-pressure acetylene gas from the acetylene cylinder and reduce the pressure to a suitable, safe working output. The regulator connects to the cylinder with a threaded inlet connection and connects to the fuel hose with a threaded outlet connection. The outlet connection is reserve threaded, tightening counterclockwise. The threads on both connections should be kept free from dirt, dust, oil, or grease. When assembled, both connections should be tightened down with a wrench.

The pressure adjusting knob on the regulator opens clockwise and closes counterclockwise. The high pressure gauge measures the pressure in the acetylene cylinder. The low pressure gauge measures the output pressure to the hose. The builder should never use the pressure adjusting knob to set the low pressure gauge beyond 15psi (1.03bar/103kpa). An output pressure of 5psi

(0.35bar/34.5kpa) is suitable for torch brazing. When finished brazing, the pressure adjusting knob should be closed.

Oxygen Regulator

The purpose of the oxygen regulator (Figures 7-2 and 7-3) is to receive high-pressure oxygen from the oxygen cylinder and reduce the pressure to a suitable, safe working output. The regulator connects to the cylinder with a threaded inlet connection and connects to the oxygen hose with a threaded outlet connection. The threads on both connections tighten clockwise and should be kept free from dirt, dust, oil, or grease. When assembled, both connections should be tightened down with a wrench.

The pressure adjusting knob on the regulator opens clockwise and closes counterclockwise. The high pressure gauge measures the pressure in the oxygen cylinder. The low pressure gauge measures the output pressure to the hose. An output pressure of 5psi (0.35bar/34.5kpa) is suitable for torch brazing. When finished brazing, the pressure adjusting knob should be closed.

Figure 7-3: *From left to right, top to bottom: acetylene regulator, oxygen regulator, Smith® Little Torch Preset Regulator Propane 249-500A.*

Preset Pressure Regulator

The *Smith Little Torch Preset Regulator Propane 249-500A* (Figures 7-2 and 7-3) costs around $50 and allows the use of propane, MAPP, or MAPP-substitute with standard oxy-acetylene welding outfits in place of acetylene and an acetylene regulator. A single bottle of propane, MAPP, or MAPP-substitute is usually sufficient to braze an entire frame and fork. The inlet connection of the regulator threads directly onto a small disposable bottle of liquefied gas. The outlet connection has reverse threads and connects to the fuel hose. The preset regulator has no pressure gauges, but the output pressure is suitable for torch brazing. The outlet valve opens counterclockwise and closes clockwise. When finished brazing, the preset regulator should be closed.

Hoses

Hoses (Figure 7-2) transport low pressure fuel and oxygen from the regulators to the torch. Hoses are measured by their inner diameter. Hoses 3/8" (9.5mm) and larger are for heavy duties, and hoses ¼" (6.4mm) or smaller are for light duties. Torch brazing thin walled steel is generally regarded as light duty. An outfit has two hoses: an oxygen hose, which is usually colored green, and a fuel hose, which is usually red. Fittings at both ends of each hose thread onto the regulator and torch. *B* fittings are the most common. The fittings on the fuel hose are usually reverse threaded. Grade *R* and *RM* fuel hoses should only be used with acetylene. Grade *T* fuel hoses are suitable for all fuel types. The *Bernzomatic Oxygen MAPP Brazing Kit* (Figure 7-2, right) has a T fuel hose.

Torch Handle

The torch handle (Figure 7-4) has two threaded connections at the bottom: one for the fuel hose (reverse threaded) and one for the oxygen hose. The two hoses should be threaded securely onto the handle using a wrench. Above each hose connection is a control knob. Oxygen and fuel mix within the body of the handle above these two valves. By opening and closing the fuel control and oxygen control knobs, the builder can fine tune the mixture of oxygen and fuel in his torch handle to arrive at the desired type of flame (discussed below). Torch handles with reverse flow check valves or flashback arrestors reduce the risk of gases mixing in the regulators or hoses, a condition that can result in a dangerous explosion. The welding tip threads onto the top of the torch handle.

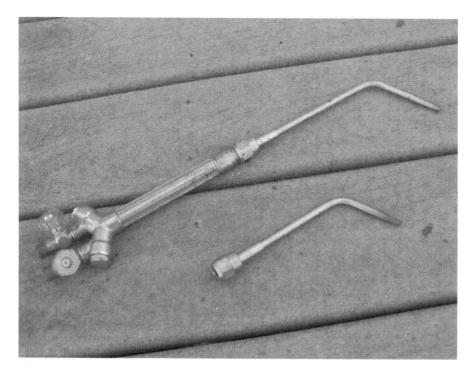

Figure 7-4: *Torch handle and welding tips. A Victor #4 welding tip is threaded on the handle. Below is a Victor #2 tip.*

Welding Tip

Cutting tips, heating tips, and welding tips thread onto the torch handle. Welding tips are the types of tips necessary for brazing bicycle forks and frames. Welding tips should be hand tightened only. A *Victor #4* tip has an opening 1.9 mm in diameter. This tip produces a large flame and works well to braze lugged and socketed joints. A *Victor #2* tip has an opening 1.2 mm in diameter and produces a small flame more desirable for fillet brazes. Victor brand welding tips (and Victor clones) work well for propane, acetylene, MAPP, and MAPP-substitute.

Oxygen Concentrator

Oxygen concentrators (figure 7-2 right) are medical devices used to treat patients with chronic obstructive pulmonary disease and other respiratory ailments. Builders can modify these machines for use with brazing torches. An oxygen concentrator uses electrical power to transform the ambient air, which is twenty-one percent oxygen, to produce an outflow gas with an oxygen purity of 85 percent or higher. For most machines, the oxygen purity of the outflow gas decreases as the flow volume increases. New, these devices cost thousands of dollars. However, used devices can be found on internet classifies such as *craigslist.com* for less than $200. Used oxygen concentrators are a cost effective alternative to refillable oxygen cylinders for hobbyists who plan on building several bicycle frames. For torch brazing, units that produce 85 percent or purer oxygen at a flow rate of 5 liters a minute are sufficient. More powerful units with flow rates beyond 5 L/min are not necessary. When used with a brazing torch, a suitable flow rate of oxygen may vary between 1.5 and 4 L/min depending on the type and brand of torch, size of the welding tip, and the mass of the metal to be heated. Not all oxygen concentrators display the output purity of oxygen as a percent.

A prospective buyer can qualitatively test a unit for function by lighting a small piece of wood, blowing out the fire so the wood remains as a smoking ember, and placing the ember near the output tube of the unit. If the unit is purifying oxygen, the ember will flare back to a flame. If nothing happens, the unit is not functioning properly. The builder can connect the medical tube to the torch hose using a barbed adaptor.

Spark Lighter

The builder should use a spark lighter to light an oxy-fuel or MAPP-air torch. Using a cigarette lighter or match is an unsafe practice.

Eye Protection

Photokeratitis, or welder's flash, is an acute painful ocular condition that occurs when a single large exposure to ultraviolet light damages the cornea. Although photokeratitis is an uncommon occurrence during brazing, cumulative exposures to low levels of ultraviolet and infrared light from the brazing torch may damage the eyes slowly over time. Glasses or goggles with a shade factor of 4 are sufficient to protect the builder during torch brazing.

Recommended Oxy-Fuel Outfits

For safety purposes, we recommend you assemble an oxy-fuel outfit that uses propane, MAPP, or MAPP-substitute rather than acetylene. If you are not using a modified version of the Bernzomatic Oxygen MAPP Brazing Kit, you will need a Smith Little Torch Preset Regulator Propane 249-500A to replace the acetylene regulator of an industrial oxy-fuel outfit. You will also require a T-grade fuel hose.

Harbor Freight sells the *Chicago Electric Welding Systems Heavy Duty Oxygen and Acetylene Welding Accessory Kit* (item #98958), which is essentially a clone of a Victor-brand outfit. For $130 to $180, this kit comes with oxygen and acetylene regulators, an R-grade hose, and a torch handle with flashback arrestors. This kit does not come with oxygen or acetylene cylinders, but you can purchase a 20-cubic-foot (566 L) oxygen cylinder directly from a welding supply store, such as Airgas. The cutting and welding tips that come with this kit are not well suited for brazing lugged frames and forks. However, for around $13 to $18, Harbor Freight sells *the Chicago Electric Welding Systems Oxygen/Acetylene Welding Tip #4* (item #99821), another Victor-brand clone.

For around $400, Airgas sells a small Victor-brand outfit complete with an R-grade fuel hose, a Victor #2 torch tip, a cutting tip, a completely filled 10-cubic-foot (283 L) acetylene cylinder, and a completely filled 20-cubic-foot (566 L) oxygen cylinder.

You should use caution if you choose to purchase a used outfit from a newspaper or online classified advertisement. Older torch handles might not have flashback arrestors. Neglected, corroded, or abused regulators, cylinders, or hoses can fail, resulting in a fire or an explosion.

General Operation of the Oxy-Fuel Outfit

Before assembling the outfit, you should inspect the threaded fittings on the hoses, regulators, cylinders, torch handle, and welding tip. Remove all traces of dust, dirt, grime, oil, grease, and other debris. Close all valves on the cylinders, regulators, and torch handle.

You should assemble the oxy-fuel outfit so that the fittings on the regulators, cylinders, and both ends of both hoses are wrench tight. Thread the welding tip finger tight upon the torch handle.

Fully open the valve on the oxygen cylinder counterclockwise. The needle on the high pressure gauge should move to indicate the pressure in the cylinder. Slowly turn the oxygen regulator valve clockwise until the low pressure gauge indicates about 5psi (0.35bar/34.5kpa). Make sure the oxygen control valve on the torch handle is completely closed.

Open the valve on the acetylene cylinder three-quarters to one and a half turns counterclockwise. The needle on the high pressure gauge should move to indicate the pressure in the cylinder. Slowly turn the acetylene regulator valve clockwise until the low pressure gauge indicates about 5psi (0.35bar/34.5kpa). Make sure the fuel control valve on the torch handle is completely closed. If you are using a preset regulator on a disposable bottle of propane, MAPP, or MAPP-substitute, there are no gauges. Open the valve of the preset regulator counterclockwise but make sure the fuel control valve on the torch handle is completely closed.

Open the fuel control valve on the torch handle one-eighth to one-quarter turns to allow fuel gas to emerge from the welding tip. Ignite the gas with the spark lighter. The flame that emerges is called the *fuel flame*. The fuel flame is orange and often produces obvious smoke and soot. Continue to open the fuel control valve until the soot and smoke disappear. With a Victor #4 welding tip, the fuel flame is around 15 to 20 cm long.

Slowly open the oxygen control valve. Opening the valve too quickly can cause the fuel flame to blow out, requiring you to start over and relight the flame. With the addition of a small amount of oxygen, the fuel flame changes to a *strongly carburizing flame* (Figure 7-5). The strongly carburizing flame has an excess of fuel gas compared to oxygen. You should see a double flame: a pale blue outer flame, and a long inner flame that is blue at the base but has a yellow or orange trailing feather. As you continue to open the oxygen control valve, the inner flame becomes shorter, loses the yellow or orange feather, and becomes blue with sharp margins. When the trailing yellow or orange feather is very small, the flame is *slightly carburizing*. At the point when the yellow or orange feather completely disappears, the flame is *neutral* (Figure 7-6), burning equal amounts of oxygen and fuel. A neutral flame or slightly carburizing flame is suitable for brazing.

Figure 7-5: *A strongly carburizing flame. The outer flame is light blue and the inner flame has an orange or yellow feather.*

Figure 7-6: *A neutral flame. The outer flame is light blue. The inner flame is dark blue, has sharp margins and no trailing orange or yellow feather.*

For educational purposes, let us assume that we continue to open the oxygen control valve after we achieve a neutral flame. The inner flame will shorten in size and come to a sharp point (Figure 7-7). This type of flame is the *oxidizing flame* and contains an excess of unused oxygen. The oxidizing flame, as the name implies, will oxidize steel surfaces and rapidly exhaust brazing flux. The oxidizing flame is not suitable for torch brazing. Oxidizing flames work well to burn paint and powder coats off steel surfaces, but the resulting fumes and vapors are unhealthy.

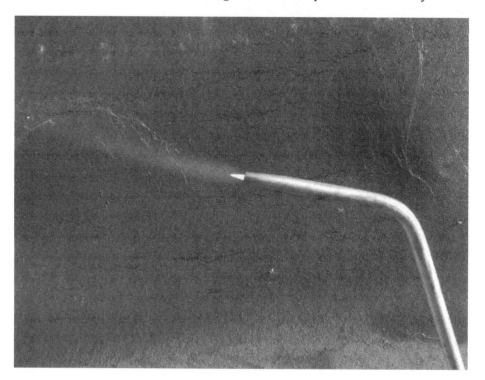

Figure 7-7: *The oxidizing flame has a short, sharp, blue inner cone.*

To turn the torch off, close the oxygen control valve on the torch handle slowly and completely. Close the fuel control valve only after closing the oxygen valve or the flame may shoot back into the torch causing a dangerous flashback. Close both cylinder valves. If you are using a preset fuel regulator, close the oxygen cylinder valve along with the preset regulator. The high pressure gauges on all regulators should go to zero, but the low pressure readings might remain unchanged. Open the oxygen control valve on the torch handle to remove pressure from the regulator and hose. The low pressure oxygen gauge on the oxygen regulator should go to zero. Close the oxygen control valve. Close the valve on the oxygen regulator counterclockwise. Open the fuel control valve on the torch handle to remove pressure from the regulator and hose. The low pressure gauge should go to zero. Close the fuel control valve. If you are using a preset regulator, the shut off process is complete. If you are using an acetylene regulator, close the regulator valve counterclockwise.

Oxy-propane and oxy-propene flames are much more difficult to adjust than oxy-acetylene flames. With propane and propene, the flame has a tendency to push off the torch tip and blow itself out. One trick to avoid this blow off effect is to start with a tiny fuel flame the size of a birthday cake candle. Alternate adding small amounts of oxygen and fuel until you reach the desired flame size and type. As the torch tip warms up, flame blow off occurs less frequently. Smaller welding tips, such as a Victor #2, are very difficult to use with propane and propene. Larger tips are preferable.

Propane and propene do not create a true neutral flame in the same manner as acetylene. For this reason, these fuels are not appropriate for fusion welding (but still work well for cutting and brazing). When using oxy-propane or propene, create a flame that more or less looks like a neutral flame and has an audible hiss. Back off the oxygen if the inner cone shortens excessively.

Adjusting the flame when using an oxygen concentrator in place of an oxygen cylinder can be tricky. Leaving the oxygen control knob on the torch handle fully open and controlling oxygen flow directly from the adjustment knob on the concentrator facilitates flame adjustment.

Chapter 8: Brazing Basics

Methods of Joining Metal Parts

The three major methods of joining steel parts together are welding, soldering, and brazing. During welding, steel structures are more or less melted together, and the filler material is the same or very similar to the parent metal of the adjoining parts. Most production frames and forks are welded using TIG (tungsten inert gas) welding machines. Although effective, TIG machines are usually too expensive for the frame or fork building hobbyist. MIG (metal inert gas) welding machines are cheaper than TIG machines. Whereas TIG welders can release heat and melt metal in a pulsed and controlled fashion, MIG welders release heat rather rapidly, which can distort or burn holes through thin-walled structures.

During soldering and brazing, the steel parts are not melted. Rather, they are joined together using a type of metal glue known as a *filler alloy*. The filler alloy is a metal that has a lower melting temperature than the steel parts, so the builder can melt the filler metal into the gap between parts without actually melting (or warping) the steel. The molten filler material fills the gap by capillary action.

In both soldering and brazing, heat performs two functions: First, the heat melts the filler material so that it can flow into the joint space. Second, the heat allows the parent metal of the frame or fork part to form a metallurgic bond with the filler alloy. If the parent metal is not heated to the right temperature, molten filler alloy will not form a strong bond.

Soldering and brazing require the use of a flux. Flux is a chemical mixture of reducing agents (usually boron or fluorides) that reduces or sequesters oxides created by heat and combustion. Without flux, a soldered or brazed joint becomes contaminated with oxides that inhibit formation of a strong metallurgic bond. As a consequence, the resulting joint would be very weak.

Soldering uses a soft filler alloy and, by definition, occurs at a temperature less than 450C (800F). Soldered joints are too weak to join bicycle frame or fork parts safely.

Brazing is essentially soldering at a higher temperature, greater than 450C (800F). The type of filler alloys used in brazing is harder and tougher than soft solder. Unlike soldering, brazed joints are adequately strong for bicycle frame and fork building.

Fillet Joints

Fillet joints are constructed for joints designed without a lug, plug, or socket. The builder lays down a ring of filler material called a *fillet* around the joint to resist sheering forces. A skilled builder can file down the fillet so that the frame or fork appears seamless after painting. Fillet joints have very little overlap between connecting steel parts, so the durability of the joint is largely dependent on the toughness of the filler alloy to resist destructive forces. The vast majority of fillet joints use brass as a filler metal because brass has a high toughness and forms fillets quite well.

Lugged Joints

Lugged (socketed) and plugged joints are designed to increase the overlap between adjacent steel parts. Joint overlap vastly increases the strength of the joint through a large surface area and by transforming tensile forces into sheering forces. The durability of a lugged (or *lap*) joint depends largely on the bonding energy between the brazing alloy and steel and much less on the inherent toughness of the brazing alloy itself.

The *joint space* is the gap between the overlapping parts. More often than not, the joint space is not visible to the builder after the joint is assembled. *Penetration* is the extent to which we fill our joint space with filler alloy. A joint completely filled with filler alloy is *completely penetrated*. A *shoreline* (which is technically a small fillet) is the presence of brazing alloy at the edges of a lug (Figure 9-3 Chapter 9). *Voids* occur when a joint is not completely penetrated. Small voids have a minimal impact on joint durability. Large voids can cause a lugged joint to fail under load.

Silver brazing alloys are frequently used for lugged joints because many formulations of silver-based alloy flow well into tight spaces, maximizing joint penetration. Silver brazing alloys contain silver and other metal elements. Silver brazing is sometimes called *silver soldering*. However, this name is technically incorrect because the filler alloy melts at temperatures over 450°C (800°F). Brass brazing alloys do not flow into tight spaces as well as most silver brazing alloys.

Recommended Brazing Alloys

The American Welding Society (AWS) designates silver brazing alloys with standards abbreviated *BAg*. (In contrast, brass alloys have the standard *RCuZn*). To successfully complete the bicycle frame procedures described in this manual, you will require a silver-based brazing alloy with the following properties:

1. The alloy should be designed for torch brazing and not vacuum-furnace brazing.

2. The alloy should be designed for use with steel.

3. In molten form, the alloy must be able to flow into tight spaces by capillary action.

4. For safety purposes, the alloy should not contain cadmium.

BAg-7 includes brand names such as *Safety-Silv 56* from the *Harris Products Group* and *Silvaloy 560 (Braze 560)* from LucasMilhaupt. This alloy meets all of the above criteria and contains 56 percent silver, 17 percent zinc, 22 percent copper, and 5 percent tin. The melting range of 1145 to 1205°F (618 to 652°C) is very narrow, which contributes to high flowing properties.

BAg-5 includes brand names such as Safety-Silv 45 from the Harris Products Group and Silvaloy 450 (Braze 450) from LucasMilhaupt. This alloy works adequately for brazing lugged, socketed, or plugged joints, but does not fill tight spaces as well as BAg-7. This alloy contains 45 percent silver, 25 percent zinc, and 30 percent copper. The melting range of this alloy (1225 to 1370°F [662 to 743°C]) is wider than BAg-7 allowing better fillet-forming properties. BAg-5 works well to braze cantilever brake bosses onto seat stays. Fillets made from BAg-5 eventually turn the color of brass. If heated slowly, BAg-5 has a tendency to separate out into high-flowing and low-flowing submixtures of elemental constituents. The eutectic (high-flowing liquid portion) does not form as durable a joint as the preseparated formulation. We can avoid this separation by using only the heat of the steel subassembly (and not the direct heat of the flame) to melt the brazing alloy.

BAg-4 includes brand names such as *Safety-Silv 40T* from the Harris Products Group. BAg-4 contains 40 percent silver, 30 percent copper, 28 percent zinc, and 2 percent tin. This alloy is very similar to BAg-5 in terms of fillet-formation properties and melting temperature range. Unlike BAg-5, BAg-4 does not have a tendency to separate out into low flowing and high flowing submixtures.

BAg-24 includes brand names such as *Safety-Silv 50N* from the Harris Products Group and *Silvaloy 505 (Braze 505)* from LucasMilhaupt. BAg-24 has brazing properties similar to BAg-7 and also works well for lugged, socketed, and plugged joints. This alloy contains 50 percent silver, 28 percent zinc, 20 percent copper, and 2 percent nickel. This alloy is not the same thing as the *nickel silver* rods available at some hardware stores (discussed below). The melting range for this alloy is 1220 to 1305°F (660 to 707°C). The small amount of nickel in BAg-24 improves bonding to stainless steel.

Used alone, any of the four brazing alloys discussed above work adequately for all brazed joints of a lugged bicycle fork. BAg-7 works best for tight sockets and plugs. BAg-5 and BAg-4 work well for loosely fitting plugs and sockets and for small fillet brazes (cantilever brake bosses). BAg-24 works best to braze stainless-steel parts.

Silver brazing alloys are sold by the troy ounce (31 g). One troy ounces should be sufficient to build an entire lugged fork. The cost of all silver brazing alloys is highly variable from year to year and depends largely on the price of the silver commodity trade. Online sources such as Amazon or EBay generally provide more affordable prices than welding supply stores such as Airgas.

The nickel-silver brazing rods found at some hardware stores have high melting temperatures, contain no elemental silver, and are not adequate substitutes for high-silver-content brazing alloys. Nickel-silver alloy is really a type of brass rod and has the AWS designation RCuZn-D. Synonyms for this alloy include *white brass* and *nickel brass*. RCuZn-D works well for fillet brazing but has difficulty penetrating the tight spaces of a lugged joint.

Low-content silver alloys (5 to 15 percent silver) are formulated to join copper and make very weak joints when used to join steel or stainless steel. These alloys have the AWS designation BCuP and are subsets of copper-phosphorus brazing alloys.

Recommended Brazing Flux

I recommend brazing flux with the following three characteristics:

1. The flux should be water soluble for ease of cleanup.

2. The flux should be formulated specifically for silver brazing.

3. The flux should be active to at least 1600°F (870°C).

4. The flux should come as a paste for easy application with a brush.

Two classes of brazing flux meet the above requirements: AWS 5.31 Type FB3A and AWS 5.31 Type FB3C. AWS 5.31 Type FB3A is generally known as *white flux* and includes products such as *Harris Stay-Silv White Flux* and *Superior No. 601 Silver Brazing Paste Flux*. AWS 5.31 Type FB3C is generally known as *black flux* and includes products such as *Harris Stay-Silv Black Flux.* White flux, as the name implies, is white in color. White contains fluorides, is active from 1050 to 1600°F (566 to 871°C), and is the flux that appears in the photographs of this manual. Black flux is usually dark brown in color, contains boron and fluorides, and is a little more expensive than white. Black is active from 1050 to 1800°F (566-982°C). Of these two fluxes, black is probably more forgiving for the first-time builder, who will likely use too much heat during brazing and risks exhausting his flux. Black works better at reducing the chromium oxide of stainless steel. Whereas white remains homogenous over time, black has solids that tend to settle out, leaving a thin liquid at the top of the container. Before application, black must be stirred vigorously to reconstitute a homogenous paste

Soldering flux purchased at a local hardware store is water soluble but is not active at the correct temperature. Soldering flux is not an adequate substitute for brazing flux. Borax-based fluxes intended for brazing with brass do not work well with high-content silver brazing alloys. I do not recommend the use of flux-coated brazing rods in place of a jar of flux paste.

Sequence of Events during Brazing

In brazing, the proper sequence of events is to clean the components of the joint, flux and assemble the joint (using fixtures or jigs if necessary), heat the joint to brazing temperature, introduce brazing alloy, slowly cool the joint, and then clean the assembly. Practice is the key to developing good brazing technique. Fortunately, brazing with low temperature, high flowing silver filler alloy is probably the easiest metal joining skill to acquire—even easier than soft soldering.

Gap Size

For most silver alloys, the strongest butt joint occurs when a gap of approximately 0.08 mm exists between the connecting parts. Smaller gaps will not allow complete penetration of filler metal and result in voids. In larger joint spaces (> 0.80 mm), the strength of the joint is determined largely by the (weaker) tensile strength of the brazing alloy rather than the (stronger) metallurgic bond between parent metal and filler alloy. High flowing silver brazing alloy will not fill very large gaps or joint spaces. However, a lugged joint is such a robust design (with large surface area overlap) and silver brazing alloys are so strong (with a tensile strength of 40,000 psi [2760 bar] or greater) that gaps larger than 0.08 mm still allow a very strong joint. When grinding out the inside of sockets, a good rule of thumb is to remove enough metal so that you do not have to strain yourself to insert the tube or blade into the socket. On the other hand, you should not remove so much metal that the tube or blade wobbles within the lug loosely. An unbrazed subassembly that is slightly too tight will yield a stronger joint than one that is slightly too loose.

Cleaning the Components of a Joint

Paint, metal burrs and filings, oil, grime, and other debris will burn and create oxides in the presence of heat. Brazing flux has a cleaning effect on the joint by sequestering oxides that can contaminate the joint and create a weak braze. However, even a generous application of flux quickly becomes exhausted if the joint is not clean prior to brazing. All surfaces need to be bright and shiny prior to brazing.

Frame and fork supply manufacturers often oil steel parts to prevent rust and corrosion. Prior to brazing, you should remove all traces of oil by rubbing the tube down with a clean rag soaked in mineral spirits. You should file off burrs and metal shards, which have high surface area and oxidize quickly, from the machined edges of fork parts. Loose debris can be simply wiped or brushed off. Paint, rust, or scale can be removed with an abrasive such as steel wool, sandpaper, or a metal brush. A grinding wheel on a rotary tool set at low revaluations is useful to clean the inner walls of tubular structures and the inner contours of sockets. Abrasive cleaning methods should only be used after oil is removed from a steel surface. Abrading an oily surface will drive oil deeper into the steel.

You can use most brands of toilet bowl cleaner that contain hydrochloric acid to remove thick scale, oxides, or other dirt not easily removed by an abrasive. Pour a small amount of toilet bowl cleaner onto the steel and spread the liquid around with a metal brush until you completely cover the stain, scale, or oxidized surface. Allow the toilet bowl cleaner to sit for a few minutes before briskly scrubbing with a wire brush. If necessary, you can repeat this sequence a second or third time until the metal surface is bright and shiny. This method will clean, in minutes, stains that cannot be scrubbed off in hours. All acid residues and the inert ingredients of toilet bowl cleaner should be completely rinsed off with water. Naval jelly (phosphoric acid) is an alternative to hydrochloric acid and is more suitable to clean stainless steel.

Applying Flux

Flux is your loyal friend. You can never use too much flux. Not using enough flux during brazing causes the flux to become quickly exhausted (completely saturated with oxides). Brazing alloy will not bond to steel through exhausted flux. If the flux becomes exhausted, you may have to cool, clean, re-flux, and re-braze the subassembly, wasting much time and effort.

As a general rule, you should flux the joining surfaces of the components of a joint (such as the outside of a tube and the inside of a socket) prior to assembly. After assembly, flux the outside of the lug and any steel within 8 cm of where you will apply heat (Figure 11-4, Chapter 11). Oxides that adhere to un-fluxed steel are more difficult to remove compared to oxides sequestered in flux.

Heating the Joint

They key to successful brazing is to use the correct amount of heat and to apply heat as evenly as possible. Too little heat will cause the steel subassembly to heat up very slowly. If the heat output of the torch is too low, you risk heating only the very edges of the joint. As a consequence, the brazing alloy may not penetrate the entire joint space, resulting in a weak joint that might fail under load.

Too much heat can have three negative consequences:

1. The flux may become exhausted before you finish brazing the subassembly. Thereafter, oxides can build up preventing the brazing alloy from properly penetrating the joint.

2. Too much heat for too long can distort steel, altering its shape. Thin walled chromoly and stainless steels are particularly susceptible to distortion.

3. Too much heat for too long alters the granular structure of steel. These granular changes can cause heat treated steels and martensitic stainless steel to lose toughness. Granular changes can cause carbide precipitation (sensitization and corrosion susceptibility) in austenitic stainless steel. Fortunately, flux usually becomes exhausted and turns black before granular alterations occur, giving us ample warning before damage takes place.

The appearance and color of the flux and steel provide the builder important clues about the temperature of the subassembly. For white flux, cool flux is white and pasty (Figure 8-1, A). As we heat our subassembly, the outer surface of the flux bubbles and takes on a dirty, globular, blobby, brown-gray appearance (Figure 8-1, B). With more heat, the brown-gray blobs become confluent and smooth and change color to clear (Figure 8-1, C). Once clear, the flux can never turn white again, even after cooling. The clear flux is active and sequesters oxides generated by the heating process. When the flux is clear, the subassembly is either right below or right at silver brazing temperature. A skilled builder will keep the flux this color for the entire brazing process. A novice, however, will likely have to apply a little more heat to ensure that the silver penetrates fully into the lugged subassembly. With additional time and heat, the flux sequesters more oxides and starts to turn yellow-green in patches (Figure 8-1, D, E). At this appearance, the silver brazing alloy should readily melt and bond to the subassembly. Unfortunately, the green appearance also means that the brazing flux is approaching exhaustion. Beyond green, the flux turns brown and then finally takes on a black, burnt appearance (Figure 8-1, F). Black, burnt-looking flux is completely exhausted. Brazing alloy cannot pass or bond through exhausted flux. If the exhausted flux occurs within the joint space (where parts overlap) or at the majority of the edge of the socket (where we would place the brazing alloy), the brazing attempt has failed. We would need to disassemble, clean, reflux, reassemble, and rebraze the subassembly. Exhausted flux elsewhere (outside the joint space or away from lug edges) will not impede the flow of brazing alloy but may indicate that the flux in the joint space is at risk of exhaustion. When flux cools, it becomes solid but retains its color (Figure 8-2).

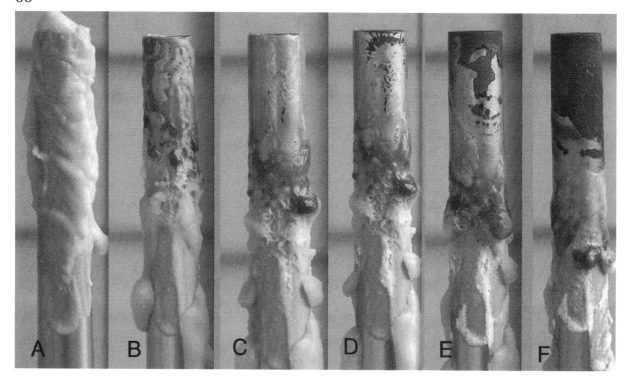

Figure 8-1. *A: Flux paste prior to application of heat. B: Prior to reaching brazing temperature, the flux has a gray globular appearance. C: At brazing temperature, the flux is clear and has a uniform texture. D: Early signs of flux exhaustion, the builder should move the blobs of flux below the clear area onto the darker patches above. E: Later signs of flux exhaustion. F: Flux completely exhausted.*

You can salvage green or brown flux. One technique is to use a clean steel edge (or even the brazing rod itself) to pick up a blob of clear molten flux elsewhere on the subassembly and place the blob in the area that is becoming dark (Figure 8-1, D, E). With heat, the blob will fuse with the dark patch and the dark patch may reverse its color. Brown flux will become green, and green flux will become clear. If large portions of the subassembly are green, brown, or black, you should stop brazing, cool the subassembly, and apply more flux. If flux becomes completely exhausted with black patches on the majority of the surface of the subassembly (Figure 8-1, F), the flux is not salvageable. The builder will have to cool the subassembly, clean, reflux, and try again.

Black flux remains active for a longer duration and at a higher temperature than white flux. Black flux resists overheating longer than white and is probably easier to use for the first-time builder. Other than the fact that black flux is dark brown when first applied, color transitions are the same as for white (clear, yellow-green, brown, crusty burnt black).

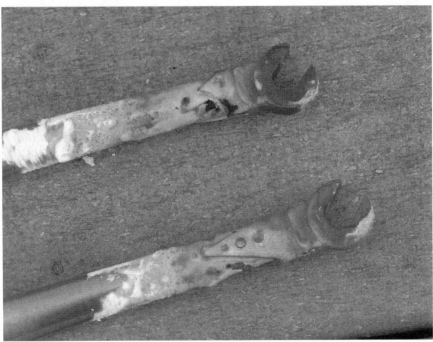

Figure 8-2: *Fork crown steering tube subassembly (top) and fork blade dropout (bottom) subassemblies shortly after brazing. Areas of active flux that were clear and watery during brazing take on a glassy appearance after the subassemblies cool. Patches of yellow, green, brown, and black flux remain the same color after cooling. The flux has turned green and brown (darker spots) in places. Overall, these subassemblies show minimal signs of overheating or flux exhaustion.*

When brazing a large piece of metal to a smaller one, you can compare the color of the flux of the two pieces for important clues about brazing temperature. If one piece (usually the smaller, less massive one) appears clear but the other piece (usually the larger, more massive one) appears grey-brown, sweaty, and globular then you should not introduce brazing alloy. The globular appearing piece is likely below brazing temperature. Brazing alloy will likely flow onto the piece with clear flux and might even appear to flow into the joint space, but the alloy will not form a good metallurgic bond with the globular appearing piece. The resulting braze will be weak and will probably fail under load. You need to make sure that the texture and color of the flux indicates that both pieces have reached brazing temperature before introducing filler alloy. Flux on the smaller piece may even begin to show signs of exhaustion before flux on the larger piece indicates brazing temperature. You should be prepared to move blobs of flux around using the method described previously. Pointing the flame primarily at the larger piece is also helpful.

In direct sunlight, steel at silver brazing temperature has no obvious glow or tint. In low light conditions (such as indoors with the lights turned down), steel at silver brazing temperature has a dull cherry-red glow. In direct sunlight, a red glow indicates the subassembly is becoming overheated. The frame builder can silver braze steel at this color, but he risks exhausting his flux. Bright red steel is too hot for silver brazing, but appropriate for brass brazing.

Placement of the Brazing Rod

The builder should use the heat of the steel and not the heat of the flame to melt the silver brazing rod. Silver brazing rods have a very small mass per unit length. A silver brazing rod placed in between the flame and subassembly will heat to melting temperature long before the steel is hot enough to permit bonding. The silver will not bond to the steel and will likely drop off the subassembly, resulting in nothing more than an expensive mess.

Controlling the Flow of Brazing Alloy through the Joint Space

Three important factors that determine the flow of molten brazing alloy are heat, gravity, and the availability of active flux. Flux, unlike brazing alloy, does not defy gravity. Eventually, flux will flow downhill from the subassembly, cool, and congeal. If necessary, you can use a clean steel edge or the brazing rod to pick up and move small pieces of this downhill reservoir onto yellow, green, or brown areas of flux uphill.

Heat is a stronger directional determinant than gravity when brazing with high-flowing silver alloy. You can draw brazing alloy upward against gravity via capillary action by heating a location uphill from where you introduce the brazing rod.

Regardless of torch type, we should always start brazing a cold subassembly with a *preheat*, heating the entire joint as evenly as possible until all flux outside the joint turns clear. After the preheat, some expert builders have the ability to use long, fluid movements of the torch to bring all areas of the joint to brazing temperature at the same time, but amateur builders usually have to concentrate the flame over a smaller area, bringing subareas of the joint to brazing temperature in a serial, piecemeal fashion. At brazing temperature, we can see silver melt and bond to steel at the edge of a lug or plug but cannot see filler alloy flow within the joint space (which is out of view). Directing heat to move molten brazing alloy across a steel surface or through a joint space is often called *sweating*. Introducing the brazing rod at one location and watching filler alloy emerge at distant edges (*sweating the alloy out*) is the key to achieving proper joint penetration. Of course, alloy will flow into only those parts of the joint that have reached brazing temperature. How we concentrate our flame and whether we introduce filler alloy at only a few points or many locations depends largely on our type of torch (discussed later).

Excess silver alloy or improper application of heat can produce a large pool or puddle of molten silver brazing alloy outside the joint space. Alloy in this location serves no purpose and requires extensive filing or standing for removal after solidification. You can avoid formation of a large pool of brazing alloy by introducing the end of the brazing rod at the edge of the socket only after the color and appearance of the flux indicates the joint has reached brazing temperature. If the joint has not reached brazing temperature, the alloy will either lump into a ball or form a pool near the side of the socket but will not flow into the joint space. At brazing temperature, heat will draw brazing alloy into the joint by capillary action. Remove the brazing rod as soon as you see the formation of *shorelines*, which are the emergence of filler alloy at the edges of a joint distant from the rod's point of placement. If you wait too long to remove the rod, the alloy will have nowhere to flow once the joint is fully penetrated and will form pools outside the joint. Ideally, you can fully penetrate the joint space and have no alloy pool beyond the small shorelines at the joint's edges (Figure 9-3, Chapter 9). However, a fully penetrated lugged joint with an adjacent pool of excess brazing alloy is more durable than an underpenetrated joint with no pool.

When we are confident that we have achieved good penetration of filler alloy throughout the entire lugged joint space, we should allow the subassembly to cool slightly, just below brazing temperature, and inspect our work. If necessary, we can reheat and rebraze any lug edges with small gaps. Sometimes, gaps in the shorelines are not apparent until after we clean the subassembly.

Brazing with a MAPP-Air Torch

The MAPP-air torch does not produce carburizing, neutral, and oxidizing flames in the same manner as an oxy-fuel torch. Although the temperature of the MAPP-air torch does not change much, the builder can change the overall heat output by opening or closing the valve regulator. A small flame (the regulator barely open) is short and quiet and puts out a small amount of heat. With the regulator nearly fully open, the MAPP-air torch puts out a long, noisy, roaring flame, and has a high heat output.

Although counterintuitive, maximum heat output does not occur with the regulator valve fully open. At full blast, the torch puts out an excess of gas compared to oxygen available in the ambient air. The MAPP gas will not burn completely, which lowers the flame's temperature. The builder may even be able to smell unburned gas. Maximum heat output occurs when the builder fully opens the MAPP-air torch valve regulator but then turns it back approximately one full rotation.

The color of a MAPP-air flame is almost always light blue and does not change much based on flame size. The builder can use the color of his MAPP-air flame as a rough measure of background light conditions. If the entire blue flame is visible, then lighting conditions are low, and the builder can use a faint red glow of the steel as a clue that the subassembly has reached brazing temperature. If only part (or none) of the blue flame is visible, then background light is high and a red glow of steel indicates the subassembly is possibly overheating.

The MAPP-air flame is much colder than an oxy-fuel flame and the two types of torches require very different movement techniques during silver brazing. You should hold the torch tip of a MAPP-air torch approximately 5 cm from the steel subassembly. At any one moment in time, the MAPP-air flame can heat to silver brazing temperature an area of steel only about 10 to 25 cm². You should, therefore, move the torch slowly, concentrating the flame over an area approximately 10to 25 cm². For larger joints, such as the lugs of the front triangle of a bicycle frame, a builder would have to braze in a serial, piecemeal fashion, introducing filler alloy at multiple points, brazing small blocks each 10 to 25 cm² until the entire subassembly is penetrated with filler alloy. Smaller joints, such as the fork blade dropout and the crown fork blade subassemblies, are often less than 10 to 25 cm² in area, requiring the builder introduce filler alloy at only one or two points.

The major drawback of brazing with a MAPP-air torch is the risk of under heating a subassembly, resulting in a poorly penetrated, weak joint. The fork crown steering tube subassembly should never be brazed with a MAPP-air torch because the flame is not hot enough to get this large mass of metal to brazing temperature. Under some conditions, the MAPP-air torch is sufficient to braze the fork crown fork blade subassemblies (Chapters 14). The MAPP-air torch is sufficient to braze the vast majority of fork blade dropout subassemblies and cantilever brake bosses.

Brazing with an Oxy-Fuel Torch

When brazing with oxy-fuel, you should use a neutral or slightly carburizing flame (Chapter 7). Large but low pressure flames work best when silver brazing lugged joints. Whereas the risk of under heating is the major drawback of a MAPP-air flame, the risk of overheating is the major drawback of an oxy-fuel flame. Many novice builders make the mistake of focusing the oxy-fuel flame over a small area of steel, causing metal to glow bright orange. Within seconds, the flux can become exhausted and turn black. Filler alloy cannot flow through exhausted flux, resulting in an underpenetrated joint. A braze performed on a subassembly overheated with an oxy-fuel flame may, therefore, be just as poorly penetrated and weak as a braze performed on a subassembly under heated with a MAPP-air flame.

To avoid overheating a subassembly, hold the tip of the oxy-fuel torch 8 to 15 cm from the subassembly. You must move the torch systematically and fluidly, applying heat as evenly as possible and avoid concentrating the flame on a single spot. Skilled builders can heat an entire subassembly evenly, introducing filler at a single location yet witnessing alloy emerge from all other edges, fully penetrating the entire joint. A technique that works well for novice builders, however, is to keep your head in a single location and heat, as evenly as possible, not the entire joint but all parts of the joint in your field of view. By introducing filler at one point, you should be able to penetrate filler alloy into the visible parts of the joint, witnessing alloy emerge from all visible edges. To finish the joint, change your point of view. Move either the subassembly or your body so that you can see those portions of the joint that were not previously visible (and not penetrated) from your initial location. Proceed again to heat all parts of the joint in your new field of view, introducing filler alloy at another point. This method will allow you to braze and completely penetrate large joints by introducing filler alloy at only two or three points. With practice, you can proceed to a more dynamic approach, constantly shifting your head, body, and point of view so that you heat the entire joint as evenly as possible and penetrate the entire joint from a single point of entry.

Tack Brazes

The builder can *tack* the parts of the subassembly in place by performing a small *tack braze*. Tack-brazing is usually performed in conjunction with some sort of jig or fixture. Tacking is simply the act of making a very small braze. Once the builder is convinced that the parts of the subassembly are in the correct position, he should make a series of small brazes about 5 mm in diameter. The builder should keep the torch pointed at the single small point where he wants to make each tack. Lug points are good places to make tack brazes. After the tacks are in place, the builder should check the alignment of his subassembly. If the angle or geometry is off, the builder can easily break the small tacks and start over. When the subassembly is tacked in the correct position, the builder can finish brazing the subassembly. If possible, the builder should keep fixtures in place. Eventually, as the builder finishes brazing the subassembly, the tack brazes melt and merge into the rest of the braze.

Brass and Nickel-Silver Brazing

Brass is a mixture of zinc and copper. Nickel-silver brazing alloy (sometimes known as white brass or nickel brass) is a variant of brass alloy, contains no elemental silver, and should not be confused with high-content silver-bearing alloy. Both brass and nickel-silver brazing alloys have high tensile strength and form large fillets well. Builders use these rods routinely to fabricate nonlugged, fillet-brazed forks and frames and for small braze-ons, such as cantilever brake bosses. Both of these kinds of brazing alloys have a higher melting temperature (around 1600 F [870 C]) than high-content silver-bearing rods. Both brass and nickel-silver require a flux active to 2000°F (1100°C). Most high-temperature brazing flux is formulated with borax. Borax is not very soluble in water, which makes cleanup difficult. Henry James sells a water-soluble flux known as *Gasflux Type B Paste* that works well for both brass and nickel-silver brazing (see references, Chapter 18).

When brazing with brass and nickel-silver, you must heat the subassembly until it glows bright orange. MAPP-air torches are insufficient to braze forks and frames with brass or nickel-silver brazing alloy; oxy-fuel torches are necessary. In the past, builders in Japan and England have use brass to braze lugged forks and frames. The technique required to perform this task is difficult because brass does not flow into tight spaces as well as silver-bearing alloys. Massive amounts of heat are required to get the entire joint to glow bright orange. Brazing lugged joints with brass or nickel-silver alloy is not covered in this manual.

Brass does not bond well to stainless steel. Nickel-silver bonds to stainless steel, but the higher brazing temperature required for this alloy often causes stainless-steel structures to distort.

Some individuals can develop a skin reaction to nickel alloys. The pathogenesis is similar to the rash of poison ivy.

Stainless Steel

I do not recommend the inexperienced builder attempt to braze stainless steel. Stainless steel is difficult to braze for several reasons. Surface chromium oxide, which prevents the alloy from rusting, inhibits formation of a metallurgic bond with brazing alloys. Chromium oxide must be removed by an abrasive technique, such as sanding, within an hour of brazing.

Stainless steel has a lower heat conductivity than non-stainless steels. A torch technique that may be adequate to heat CRMO or mild steel evenly may heat stainless steel irregularly, causing some parts of the stainless joint to overheat and others parts to remain below brazing temperature. A common result is irregular penetration of brazing alloy as well as distortion.

Stainless steel has a higher coefficient of thermal expansion than CRMO or mild steel. The difference in expansion is generally not an issue when a non-stainless part is placed into the interior of a stainless structure or socket. However, when a stainless part is placed into the interior of a non-stainless structure, the excess expansion of the stainless part during brazing may occlude the joint space, preventing penetration of filler alloy.

Carbide precipitation (sensitization) predisposes to corrosion and occurs when austenitic stainless steel is heated to temperatures above 1400F (760C) for a prolonged period of time. This temperature is within the range of silver brazing. Therefore, stainless steel structures must be brazed quickly.

The temperature at which silver bearing alloys bond to stainless steel is higher than for CRMO or mild steel. The higher temperature required to braze stainless steel causes flux to reach exhaustion quickly. Black flux works better with stainless steel than White.

Most high content silver bearing rods work sufficiently well with stainless steel, but BAg-24 (Safety-Silv 50N) probably flows the best across stainless surfaces.

Heat Treated Alloys

Heat treatments, such as quenching, tempering, and annealing, can increase the toughness of stainless steel and some low-alloy steels. Manufacturers can use heat-treated steels to fabricate lightweight frame and fork parts with very thin walls (< 0.6 mm). Thin-walled structures distort easily when heated unevenly. Furthermore, overheating can reverse some of the effects of heat treatment, weakening the steel. I, therefore, do not recommend the inexperienced builder attempt to braze heat-treated or other very thin-walled steel structures.

Brazing Location

Brazing outdoors provides maximum ventilation and minimizes the builder's exposure to flux residues, metal fumes, and combustion products. However, slight breezes can cool a subassembly, hindering the brazing process. After brazing, a breeze can cool the subassembly too quickly, embrittling the steel. An oxy-fuel torch is nearly impossible to operate outdoors. MAPP-air torches function adequately outdoors unless a breeze is very strong.

Brazing indoors allows the builder better control over lighting and ambient temperature and eliminates breezes. However, if ventilation is poor, the builder's exposure to flux residues, metal fumes, and combustion products is maximized.

Removing Flux from a Brazed Subassembly

After brazing, flux contains reactive reducing chemicals and sequestered oxides that can corrode a subassembly. You must remove these chemicals as soon as possible. First, the subassembly needs to cool slowly to room temperature. Quenching a hot subassembly in water can embrittle the steel. When the steel has cooled, you can soak the subassembly in a bucket of water. Hot or warm water removes water-soluble flux faster than cold water (Figure 8-3). Although the subassembly can literally rust before your eyes during this process, this rust is superficial and easily removed with an abrasive. Large blobs of flux can be scraped off with a metal brush or blade of a tool.

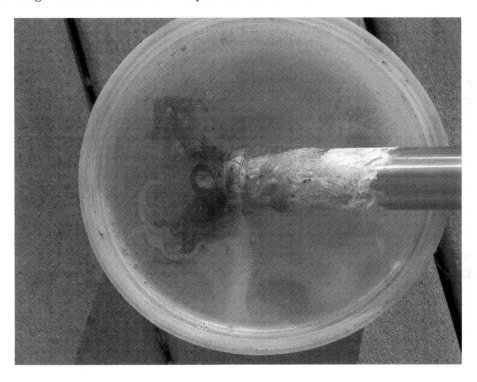

Figure 8-3: *Water will dissolve water-soluble flux after brazing.*

If you cannot fit the subassembly into a bucket of water, an alternative is to pour hot water onto the subassembly. Place about 500 ml (a pint) of water into a microwavable container and heat the container in the microwave for 3 minutes. The water may superheat, reaching a temperature higher than the boiling point but lacking a nidus to form gas bubbles. Agitate the container by bumping it with a utensil. The water will boil over if superheated, and you would prefer this occurs in the microwave rather than in your hands. If not superheated, relocate the container to your workspace. Pour a small amount of the hot water onto the subassembly and scrub with a wire brush. The flux should dissolve quickly. Repeat pouring and scrubbing until all traces of flux are gone.

You can remove exhausted flux, oxides that adhere to unfluxed steel, and rust with hydrochloric acid (found in some toilet bowl cleaners) or phosphoric acid (naval jelly) and a wire-bristled brush. Phosphoric acid is preferred to clean stainless steel. The chlorides of hydrochloric acid can leach out chromium at the surface of stainless steel, diminishing corrosion resistance.

Cleaning Shorelines

Shorelines are brazing alloy at the edges of a lug (Figure 9-3, Chapter 9). Good shorelines are a mark of good craftsmanship. You should inspect shorelines after cleaning a brazed joint. Ideally, shorelines should be concave, hug the adjacent lug edge, should not occur as large blobs or pools, and should not contain gaps. Better brazing technique and better torches generally yield better shorelines. The piecemeal approach necessary when brazing with a MAPP-air torch usually creates shorelines with small gaps and confluent blobs of brazing alloy. When gaps are present in the shoreline, you should probe them with a sharp tool to make sure they do not extend more than a few millimeters beyond the lug's edge. If probing reveals a large void, you should rebraze the subassembly.

To fill small gaps at lug edges, use a small flame and concentrate the flame on the gap. Briefly introduce the brazing rod when the shoreline adjacent to the gap starts to melt. You can file excess braze from a shoreline using the edge of a half-round file, needle file, or a rat-tailed file. Rotary tools are less effective than files at removing excess brazing alloy from the shoreline of lugged joints.

How to Practice

You need to practice and become comfortable with silver brazing before you begin building a fork. To practice brazing lugged joints, you should acquire fat and thin scrap pieces of steel to create mock lugs. The tubes do not need to be long. To practice brazing with a MAPP-air torch, the tubes should have a wall thickness around 1 mm. To practice brazing with an oxy-fuel torch, you should create two sets of mock lugs, one with thin walled (1 mm) steel tubes, and one with thick walled (3 mm or 1/8") tubes. The thick walled mock lug is similar to the fork crown steering tube subassembly. The thin walled mock lug is similar to the other fork subassemblies.

Cut off a 3 to 4 cm section of tube and cut it lengthwise to make a split ring. The split ring will fit snugly over the parent tube. You should clean and flux the assembly. Practice heating and brazing these types of mock lugged subassemblies, placing the silver brazing rod at one edge of the split ring and drawing alloy into the gap between the two tubes all the way through to the opposite edge. After brazing, cut your mock lugged joint into several pieces with a hacksaw to check the extent of the penetration of brazing alloy. When you can fully penetrate the mock-lugged joint with brazing alloy without exhausting your flux, you have achieved a basic level of proficiency in silver brazing.

Chapter 9: The Steering Tube Fork Crown Subassembly

Considerations and Pitfalls

The joint between the steering tube and fork crown experiences large mechanical stresses during a bicycle ride, especially during high impact bumps like potholes. If the steering tube fork crown subassembly is not brazed properly, the resulting fork will be weak and may fail under load, causing the rider to wreck and sustain injury or death. The steering tube and crown are made from thick walled steel to withstand mechanical stresses. This joint, therefore, must be brazed with an oxy-fuel torch to reach brazing temperature. The MAPP-air flame simply lacks the heat output to bring the subassembly to silver brazing temperature. Before the builder attempts to assemble the steering tube fork crown subassembly, he should read and understand Chapters 7 and 8, become familiar with the operations and settings of his oxy-fuel torch, and have successfully performed practice brazes on thick walled (3 mm or 1/8") steel.

Procedure for Constructing the Steering Tube Fork Crown Subassembly

1. Inspect your steering tube. If you have a threaded tube, the unthreaded end will insert into the crown. A keyway through the threads (if present) will face the back of the bicycle. If the tube has no threads, locate the butted end, which has a larger wall thickness and smaller inner diameter than the non-butted end. The thicker butt inserts into the crown.
2. Inspect your fork crown. If the crown has not been pre-drilled to mount a caliper brake, drill the hole now. Even if you plan on using cantilever or V-brakes instead of caliper brakes, the hole in the crown will allow you to mount fenders or other bike parts and is an excellent place to introduce brazing alloy during brazing. Place the crown securely in a vise so that you can access the front. Place a few drops of cutting oil on the area to be drilled. Drill a small hole using a small (1/8" or 3 mm) titanium nitride bit, a slow drill speed setting, and firm downward pressure. Flip the crown over and drill the back of the crown. Repeat the process with 4 mm, 5 mm, and 6 mm bits until you can fit the 6mm bit all the way through the crown (Figure 9-1). If you cannot obtain metric drill bits and want to mount a caliper brake, enlarge the hole to 3/16" (4.76 mm). You can use a hand reamer later to enlarge the hole to 6 mm (Chapter 14). If you cannot locate metric bits and do not plan on using a caliper brake, enlarge the hole to ¼" (6.35 mm). Use the round edge of your file to remove any burs from the inside of the steering tube socket created during the drilling process. Do not drill the steering tube at this point in time.
3. Attempt to fit the appropriate end of the steering tube into the crown. Most crowns have steering tube sockets fabricated to very tight tolerances, so the tube will likely fit well with very little wiggle or slop. If the socket is too tight to fit the steering tube, grind out the socket with a rotary tool and grinding bit. Grind out as little metal as possible until the steering tube fits snugly.
4. Remove all dirt, markings, rust, scale, or traces of oil from the outside and inside of the crown and steering tube. Use an abrasive and toilet bowl cleaner if necessary. Apply a liberal amount of flux to the end of the steering tube and the inside of the socket of the crown.

Figure 9-1: *Drill the brake caliper mounting hole into the fork crown before brazing. Even if you have no intention of using caliper brakes, this hole is an excellent location to introduce brazing alloy during brazing.*

5. Place the steering tube in the vise so that the top points downward, and place the crown on the bottom end of the steering tube (Figure 9-2). If you have a threaded tube, orient the keyway (if present) with the center of the back of the crown.
6. Apply a liberal amount of flux to the outside of the crown, including the fork blade sockets.
7. Place the inclinometer along the side of the steering tube, loosen the vise jaws, and re-orient the steering tube until it is perpendicular to the ground (Figure 9-2, top). Retighten the jaws.
8. Place the inclinometer on top of the points of the fork blade sockets of the crown. If necessary, tilt the crown upon the steering tube until the crown is parallel to the ground (Figure 9-2, bottom). (Note: if the steering tube socket of the crown is an uninterrupted bore with no lip, inclinometer measurements are of no value. Orient the crown and steering tube horizontally in the vise so that the wide axis of the crown appears to run perpendicular to the steering tube. A few millimeters of steering tube should extend beyond the bottom of the crown).

Figure 9-2: *Using an inclinometer to orient the steering tube perpendicular to the ground (top) and the crown parallel to the ground (bottom). If these parts are not oriented properly, fork alignment will suffer.*

9. Assemble your oxy-fuel torch to the appropriate settings (Chapter 7 and 8). If the crown fits loosely on the steering tube, perform a small tack braze (Chapter 8). Recheck your alignment with the inclinometer after the tack braze, breaking the braze and re-tacking if necessary.

10. Using a large (but low pressure) neutral or slightly carburizing flame, pre-heat the entire subassembly until the flux on the outside of the crown turns clear.

11. Orient yourself so that you face the front of the fork. Concentrate the flame on the front of the crown, moving the flame from side to side to evenly heat the entire front half of the outside of the crown's steering tube socket. (You need not heat the fork blade sockets). Periodically place the brazing rod into the brake mounting hole. If the rod does not melt within a few seconds, withdraw the rod and continue to heat the front of the crown. If the rod melts when placed into the hole, inspect the small gap between the steering tube and crown race below. If you do not see brazing alloy emerge from this location, withdraw the rod and continue to heat the front half of the socket as evenly as possible; you have not yet brought the entire front half of the socket to brazing temperature. Repeat heating and rod placement until brazing alloy has emerged from between the crown race and steering tube at the entire front (half-circular cross section) of the steering tube.

12. Reorient yourself so that you face the back of the subassembly. Repeat step 11 for the back of the subassembly. (If you are positioning the subassembly horizontally, flip the subassembly over so that the back faces upward. Wear protective gloves, and be careful not to burn yourself).

13. Allow the steel to cool and inspect your subassembly. If the subassembly is brazed correctly, you should have introduced brazing alloy at only two locations yet see complete rings of brazing alloy (shorelines) at the edges of the joint (Figure 9-3). If either ring of brazing alloy is interrupted, voids are present and penetration of filler alloy into the joint is not complete. If voids are present in the shoreline, repeat steps 11 and 12. If the flux has started to turn black, clean and reflux the subassembly before your second brazing attempt.

14. Remove residual flux with hot water, a wire brush, and/or toilet bowl cleaner. If the steering tube socket of the crown was an uninterrupted bore without a lip, file down edges of protruding steering tube flush with the contours at the bottom of the crown.

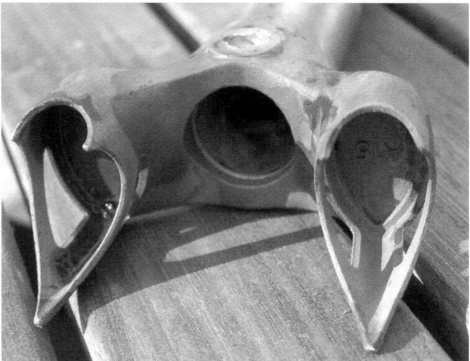

Figure 9-3: *Steering tube fork crown subassembly after brazing and preliminary cleaning. If brazed properly, you should see an uninterrupted ring of brazing alloy (light colored metal) at the edges (shorelines) of the joint. If one or both of these rings is interrupted, a void in the braze is present.*

Chapter 10: Cutting the Small Ends of the Fork Blades (Optional)

Considerations and Pitfalls

The average uncut fork blade measures between 380 and 400 mm long. Were the builder to simply braze on the fork crown and dropouts without cutting down the blades, the resulting fork would have a crown-to-axle length in excess of 410 mm. A fork of this size is generally too long for most road and cyclocross applications, resulting in a bicycle with a slack head angle and long fork trail. Cutting a fork blade down from the large end is generally simpler than cutting from the smaller end and results in a supple fork with good shock absorbing properties. If the builder wishes to cut only from the large end of the blade, he can skip this section of the book entirely and should perform his cut after bending his blades (if necessary). Cutting the fork blade down to size from the small end makes for a more rigid, stiffer fork more suitable for harder use such as cyclocross.

Cutting from the small end of the fork blade may complicate future placement of socketed or plugged dropouts depending on the location of the blade's taper. If the builder cuts too high into the taper, he may find the dropout socket or plug is too small to fit properly at the small end of the blade. However, this problem with dropout fit is seldom an issue for forks with intended crown-to-axle lengths of 375 mm or longer because the cut will be rather short and should not extend too far into the taper.

Cutting from the small ends must be performed before the blades are bent; otherwise, arriving at the correct fork rake becomes difficult. However, any cut in the blade prior to bending complicates achieving the desired crown-to-axle length. Often, a smaller (<1 cm) second cut from the large end of the blade is necessary after bending to fine tune the crown-to-axle length.

Procedure for Cutting the Small Ends of the Fork Blades

1. Examine the inside of the fork blade sockets of the crown to determine where the top of the fork blades will lie once inserted. Mark the approximate location on the outside of one of the sockets.
2. Place the fork crown on a level surface. Using a tape measure held parallel to the vertical axis of the crown, measure the distance from the bottom of the crown race to the mark made in step 1 above. Record this distance as the *crown-to-blade-top distance* in mm. For most crowns this measurement will lie somewhere between 5 and 40 mm and depends largely on shoulder slope.
3. Examine the dropouts to determine where the very end of the fork blades will lie once placed on/in the blade. If the dropout is socketed, mark the approximate location on the outside of the socket. If the dropout is plugged, no mark is required as the top of the lip is present at this location.
4. Measure from the center of the slot to either the top of the lip (plugged dropouts) or the mark from step 3 above (socketed dropouts). Record this distance as the *dropout length* in mm. Typical values range from 10 to 30 mm.
5. Subtract the sum of the dropout length and crown-to-blade-top distances from the desired crown-to-axle length. The result is an approximation of the desired *post-cut blade length*.

(This approximation will be more accurate for forks with smaller rakes). For example, if you want a 390 mm crown-to-axle length, and your crown-to-blade-top distance and dropout length are 30 mm and 10 mm, respectively, your post-cut blade length would be: 390 mm – (30 mm + 10 mm) = 350 mm.

6. Measure the uncut fork blade from end to end along the long axis. Record this number as the *precut blade length*.
7. Subtract the post-cut blade length from the precut blade length. Record this number as the *small-end cut*. For example, if your precut blade length is 390 mm and your post-cut blade length is 350 mm, the small-end cut would be: 390 mm – 350 mm = 40 mm.
8. Lay one of the fork blades on a flat surface, measure from the small end along the long axis, and mark the location of the small-end cut (Figure 10-1).

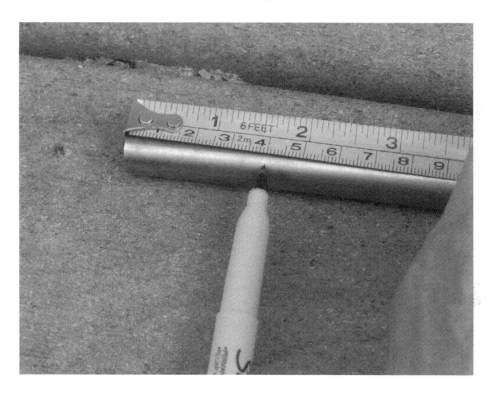

Figure 10-1: *Measuring and marking the small-end cut of the fork blade.*

9. Using a hacksaw, cut the fork blade off at the mark made in step 8 above. Steering tube cutting guides generally do not fit properly on the small ends of fork blades. However, an old flat file (or other piece of flat stock metal) placed within the guide and beneath the blade often allows the use of the cutting guide to make the cut. Otherwise the cut will have to be performed freehanded. Try to cut as perpendicular as possible to the long axis and as parallel as possible to the cross section to achieve a *square end*.
10. Place the uncut fork blade on a level surface and place the cut fork blade on top of the long fork blade. Align the large ends and the long axes of the two blades, and mark on the longer blade the location that corresponds to the cut end of the short blade.
11. Cut the long blade at the mark made in step 10 using the method described in step 9.

12. Placed the two cut blades next to one another, aligning the long axes and large ends. More likely than not, one blade will be longer than the other by a few millimeters. Mark the short blade with an *S*.

13. Inspect the cut end of the *S* blade. If the cut is not parallel to the cross section and/or not at a ninety degree angle to the long axis, touch up the end with a file until these parameters have been achieved. We will call this procedure, *filing the cuts square* and the proper result of this procedure a *square end* or *square cut*.

14. Inspect the cut end of the longer blade. If needed, file the cut square as described in step 13.

15. Compare the two blade lengths again as described in step 12. Mark the longer blade with an *L*. Depending on how *square* the initials cuts were, it is possible that the *S* blade is now the *L* blade.

16. File the small end of the *L* blade using the flat surface of a file. With each file stroke apply even pressure to the entire circular cross section. This technique will help to preserve the square-ness of the end as you file it down. Stop periodically to compare the blade lengths and continue filing until the two blade lengths are identical.

Chapter 11: Brazing the Dropouts onto the Fork Blades

Considerations and Pitfalls

Compared to bending fork blades or brazing the steering tube fork crown subassembly, brazing the dropouts onto the fork blades is a relatively simple process. If you wish to cut from the small ends of your fork blades, you need to perform this task before brazing on the dropouts. You should properly orient your dropouts onto the fork blades to the best of your ability, but if one of the dropouts is miss-rotated a few degrees, the effect on fork alignment is minimal because the dropout will flex slightly when the quick release skewer that holds the front wheel in place is closed. Part of the dropout alignment process involves preparing the fork blade sockets of the crown for final assembly.

The combination of mass, wall thicknesses, tube width, and other factors that affect thermal conductance usually permits the builder to use a MAPP-air torch to braze on the dropouts. Of course, an oxy-fuel torch would work just as well if not better.

An important pitfall to avoid is a dropout with a socket or plug that fits too loosely on the blade. A loose fit can occur if the builder purchased the wrong sized dropouts or cut the small ends of the fork blades too high into the taper. Gap size between the two component parts of a subassembly is an important determinant of the final durability of a brazed joint. If the dropout flops around loosely on the end of the blade, the builder should make measurements with calipers: For lugged dropouts, the builder should measure the inside diameter of the socket and the outside diameter of the small end of the blade. For plugged dropouts, the builder should measure the outside diameter of the plug and the inside diameter of the small end of the blade. Within each set of measurements, gap size of the joint is one-half of the difference of the two measured diameters. If the difference between the two measurements (twice the gap size) is 0.5 mm or smaller, the final joint should be adequately durable provided the dropout sockets or plugs are long (around 1 cm).

Procedure for Brazing the Dropouts onto the Fork Blades

1. Place the dropouts on the ends of the fork blades. If the sockets are too tight or the plugs too big to fit, grind the dropouts to size using a rotary tool or a file. You should only have to grind off a small amount of metal (tenths of millimeters). Do not grind the blades. You should err on the side of a fit that is too tight rather than too loose.
2. On the dropouts, clean the insides of the sockets or outsides of the plug by sanding with an abrasive (Figure 11-1). The entire joining surface should shine when adequately clean.

Figure 11-1: *Using a rotary tool with a sanding mandrel to clean the inside of the socket of a dropout. When clean, the entire joining surface should shine.*

3. Attempt to fit your fork blades into the fork crown. In most cases, the fork blade sockets of the crown are cast to much looser tolerances than the steering tube socket, so the fork blades will probably not fit properly. Sockets that are too tight are more common than sockets that are too loose. If the fit is too loose, bend the walls and points of the sockets inward using long nose pliers to tighten the fit. If the fit is too tight, either the large ends of the fork blades or the sockets will need to be modified. Determine the source of the obstruction: Compare the long and short axes of the cross section of the blades to those of the sockets, if you increase the length of one axis of the blade but decrease the other, will the blade fit? If so, change the shape of the large end of the fork blade by compression in a vise. Pinching along the long axis of the cross section will decrease the long axis and lengthen the short axis. Compressing along the short axis has the opposite effect. If pinching the blade will not (or does not) result in good fit, grind out the inside of the sockets with a rotary tool and grinding bit until the blades fit (Figure 11-2). If the socket is oval or teardrop in cross sectional shape, a smaller grinding bit may be necessary to fit into narrow sections. Grind out as little metal as possible. You should err on the side of a fit that is too tight instead of too loose. Never grind metal off the walls of the blades.

Figure 11-2: *Grinding out the inside of the fork blade sockets of the crown using a rotary tool with a grinding bit. In this instance, a smaller grinding bit is necessary to fit into and grind out the point of the cross sectional teardrop (at the back of the crown). Always determine if the blades can be made to fit by deforming the cross section in a vise before resorting to grinding the socket. Never grind the blades themselves.*

4. Create a dummy axle using your measuring tape and threaded rod: Thread four nuts down your 3/8" or 9 mm threaded rod so that the outer surfaces of the outer two nuts are 100 mm apart (Figure 11-3). This distance of 100 mm corresponds to the over locknut dimension (OLD) of most modern bicycle front wheel hubs. Place a wrench on an outer nut and another wrench on the adjacent inner nut. While securing the outer nut, tighten the inner nut against the outer nut to lock the outer nut in place. Repeat this process with the other pair of nuts at the other end of the dummy axle. Double check that the outer surfaces of the two outer nuts are spaced 100mm apart. Make adjustments if necessary.

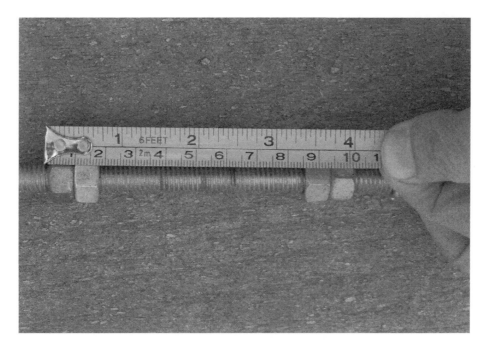

Figure 11-3: *Creating a dummy axle. The outer surfaces of the outer nuts should be 100mm apart. The inner nuts lock the outer nuts in place.*

5. Clean the outsides and insides of the small ends of the fork blades. Flux the fork blades and dropouts. Place the dropouts onto the fork blades.
6. Place the large ends of the blades into the fork blade sockets of the crown.
7. Place the steering tube into a vise so that the dropouts point upward.
8. Place the dummy axle in the dropouts (Figure 11-4). Move the fork blades back and forth, pivoting the large ends within the sockets of the crown, until the dummy axle appears to be parallel to the wide axis of the fork crown. You can estimate the orientation of the dummy axle relative to the fork crown based on appearance alone. Actual measurements are not necessary. Secure the dummy axle in place with a third pair of nuts, one on the outside of each dropout (Figure 11-4). Tighten down the outermost nuts with a wrench.

Figure 11-4: *The dummy axle holds the dropouts in place during brazing.*

9. Apply additional flux if necessary and tack braze the dropouts in place. If the dropouts are socketed, tack braze the longest point of each dropout to the fork blade. If the dropouts are plugged, pick an outside location for the tack, right below the lip of each dropout.

10. Braze in one of your dropouts. If possible, introduce filler alloy at only one or two locations, applying heat to draw brazing alloy out from all joint edges. If the dropout is socketed, introduce filler at a high location near the top of the slot. If the dropout is plugged, introduce filler right below the plug's lip.

11. Braze the other dropout in place, using the directions from step 10.

12. Allow the subassemblies to cool. Remove the fork blades from the crown and clean the dropouts by soaking them in hot water and by scrubbing with a wire brush (Figure 11-5). Remove the subassemblies from the water and tip them upside down. If water drips out from the inside of one of the fork blades, penetration of filler alloy is incomplete and a void is present in the braze. Clean the subassembly and then re-braze the affected dropout using the directions from steps 6 through 10 above to eliminate the void.

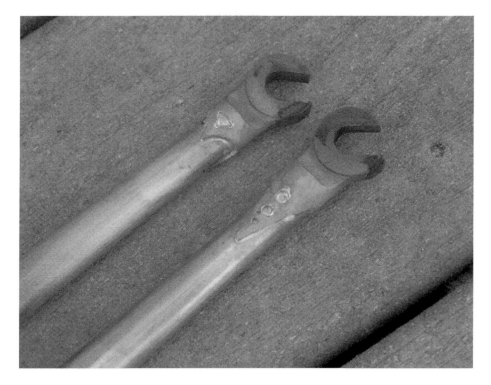

Figure 11-5: *Dropout fork blade subassemblies after brazing and brief cleaning. The lighter colored metal at the shorelines is brazing alloy. The dark stains at the ends of the slots can be removed by scrubbing with toilet bowl cleaner and a wire brush.*

Chapter 12: Bending Fork Blades

Straight Bladed Forks, Considerations

Bending a fork blade is one of the more difficult tasks in the lugged fork fabrication process. A builder who wishes to invest in less equipment can omit the step entirely by using a fork crown in which the blade sockets are offset 6 or 7 degrees relative to the steering tube. The rake of a straight bladed fork can be estimated by the following equation:

Fork rake = sine (offset angle) x (post-cut blade length + dropout length)

The offset angle is typically 6 or 7 degrees, resulting in a rake somewhere between 40 and 50 mm, with larger values for longer forks. Chapter 10, steps 1 through 5 of *Procedure for Cutting the Small Ends of the Fork Blades* explains how to estimate post-cut blade length and dropout length. The estimation method for post-cut blade length as a means to arrive at the correct crown-to-axle length is actually more accurate for straight blades than for bent blades. Although the procedure in Chapter 10 was intended for fork blades cut at the small end, the estimated value for post-cut blade length is valid for straight bladed forks cut at either end.

Pre-Bent Blades, Considerations and Pitfalls

Some manufacturers, such as Reynolds Technology, fabricate fork blades that are already bent for the builder. Such blades usually come in either 30 mm or 45 mm rakes. The builder will not be able to cut these types of blades at the small end without altering the rake significantly. Cutting these blades at the large end will not affect rake.

Bending Fork Blades, Consideration and Pitfalls

The procedures below assume we will use the homemade tube bending mandrel to bend fork blades (Chapter 6). In the event you have acquired a different bender, you may have to deviate from the procedures below to incorporate any directions, which accompany your equipment, that conflict with steps in this manual's protocols.

The builder will find it easier to make bends near the small end of the fork blade than at the large end. For any given desired fork rake, the lower the bend occurs along the fork blade, the larger the bend (camber) required to achieve the desired rake. Modern forks generally have a small bend near the top of the fork, so the method described in this manual, which places a bend near the bottom, will result in a fork with a bit of a retro look. The closer the dropout rest lies relative to the mandrel body, the lower the bend.

Prior to bending the fork blades, the builder must make a rake measuring and freeze water into the fork blades. Freezing water into the blades is not necessary but will result in less distortion during the bending.

Procedure for Making a Rake Measuring Tool

1. Tape two pieces of standard sized printer paper end to end so that the resulting rectangle measures in the ballpark of 20 cm x 50 cm.
2. Place a large hardcover book (such as a textbook) on top of the paper so that the long side of the book runs parallel to the long side of the paper and the short side of the book runs parallel to the short side of the paper. There should be 4 cm margins between the edges of the book and the edges of the paper.
3. Trace the long and short sides of the book onto the paper, creating two lines at a right angle. If the long side of the book measures less than 40 cm, extend the line to this distance using a ruler as a straight edge.
4. Measure the desired rake from the corner of the right angle along the shorter of the two lines. Mark this distance. The resulting tool should resemble Figure 12-1.

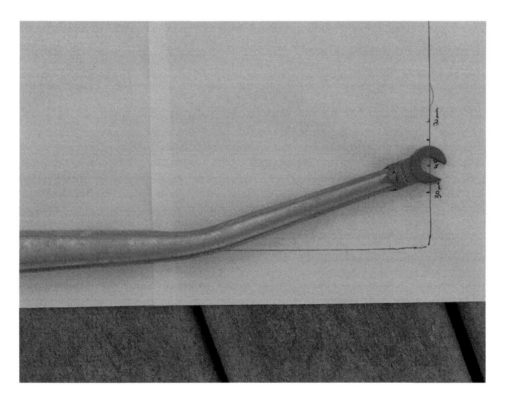

Figure 12-1: *The rake measuring tool is simply a long piece of paper with a right angle traced upon it. The builder should mark the desired target rake, 45 mm in this example.*

Procedure for Freezing Ice into the Fork Blades (Optional)

1. Holding the fork blades small ends down, pour water into the large ends of the blades, completely filling the interior. If you performed your braze properly in the last chapter, the joint between the dropout and fork blade should be completely water tight.
2. Place the fork blades into your freezer large ends pointing up. It may be necessary to tilt the blades to get them to fit. You might spill a small amount of water, which is of no

consequence because the ice will expand as it freezes and will fill the void. Allow the water to freeze overnight.

Procedure for Bending the Fork Blades

1. If you froze water into your blades, remove them from the freezer and make sure the water is completely frozen. Return the blades to the freezer if necessary.
2. Place the mandrel assembly upon a sturdy, flat surface.
3. Place one of the fork blades in the tube bender and secure the dropout upon the dropout rest of the mandrel assembly. The opening of the slot should point forward and away from the wooden mandrel body.
4. Lay the fork blade backwards into the grove of the wooden mandrel body (Figure 12-2).
5. Try to rotate the blade around its long axis. If the blade can rotate, you risk making a bend that bows either outwards or inwards. Use nuts on the dropout rest to prevent this rotation. Because most dropouts are angled relative to the fork blade, the nuts will not lie completely flush against the sides of the dropout unless the fork blade is allowed to deviate to an angle and out of the grove. Your objective is simply to restrict the rotational movement of the blade. One nut will contact the bottom of the dropout and the other will contact the top.

Figure 12-2: The blade is placed into the mandrel assembly. The tubular lever is placed upon the large end of the fork blade.

6. Locate your tubular lever. (The recommended dimensions of this lever are described in Chapter 6). Place the lever on the large end of the fork blade so that entire large end of the

tube is contained within the lever. Only the taper, small end, and dropout should be visible outside the lever (Figure 12-2).

7. To immobilize the mandrel assembly and to create additional leverage, stand with one foot on each of the two aluminum angles at the back end of the mandrel assembly.

8. To bend to fork blade, pull the tubular lever toward you using a firm but steady movement. Be sure to pull the lever straight back and not out to the side or you will create an outward bow in the blade. Pay close attention to the dropout throughout the bending process. If at any time the dropout shifts or rotates upon the rest, stop bending immediately or the bend will bow out to the side. You will have to guess when you have achieved the correct rake. Err on the side of bending too little rather than too much.

9. Remove your lever from your fork blade and your fork blade from the mandrel assembly.

10. Place your fork blade upon your rake measuring tool. The longer line should transect the midline of the large end of your fork blade. The middle of the dropout slot should lie upon the shorter line (Figure 12-1). If you are within 5 mm of your desired rake, made no additional bends to your fork blade. With each additional bend you risk bowing your fork blade out to the side. If your rake is bigger than desired, there is, unfortunately, no simple way to correct this problem using the tools described in this manual. You will either have to start over with a new blade or live with the result. (I recommend the latter). If your rake is more than 5 mm smaller than desired, repeat steps 3 through 10 until you are satisfied with the result.

11. Repeat steps 3 through 9 with your remaining fork blade.

12. Place the two fork blades next to one another on a flat surface so that the long axis of the two large ends are parallel (Figure 12-3). Inspect the orientation of the long axes of the two small ends. If the small ends are not parallel, one fork blade has been bent more than the other. Place the blade with the smaller bend in the mandrel. Repeat steps 3 through 9 above and then compare the two fork blades again. Repeat this process until the two fork blades are bent at the same angle.

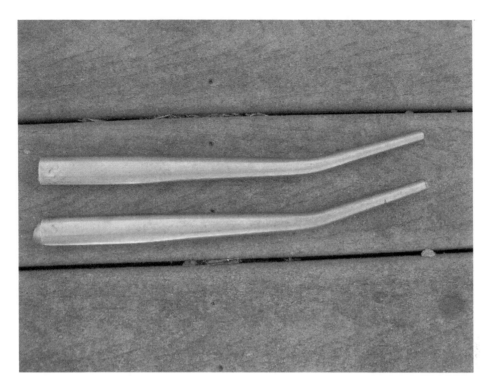

Figure 12-3: *When both blades have been bent, place them next to one another so that the large ends are parallel. Inspect the small ends. If the small ends are not parallel, re-bend the blade with the smaller angle. Note that the bending process slightly flattens the contours of the fork blade at the front of the bend. This deformation will be more pronounced if the ice freezing procedure is omitted.*

Trouble Shooting

If you overshoot or undershoot your rake by just a few millimeters, do not worry. The effect on bicycle handling and steering will be minimal. If you overshoot your rake by more than 5 mm, there might be a noticeable effect on handling.

You want a bend that is purely front to back along the fork blade. If an outward bend occurs, you have several options:

1. Live with it. Unless the angle of the side-to-side bend is large, you should be able to properly align the dropouts relative to the crown. However, one of the fork blades will bow inward or outwards relative to the plane of the wheel. Although such a fork might appear peculiar, the bowed blade should not affect steering.

2. Re-ovalize the cross section of the large end of the blade: Make two marks at the top edges of the large end to denote the desired orientation of the long axis of the cross section. These marks should lie in the same plane as the bend and should be a few millimeters offset from the current long axis. Place the large end horizontally in the vise and compress along the current long axis to transform the cross section to a circular shape. Reorient the large end in the vise so that the line that connects the two marks runs perpendicular to the vise jaws. Compress the vise to re-ovalize the large end with a new long axis that lines up with the bend. You may need to un-braze, reorient, and re-braze the dropout to compensate for the

new partial rotation of the fork blade. (This procedure is not effective for blades with teardrop shaped cross sections.)

3. Completely round fork blades have radial symmetry throughout their cross sections, so correcting for an outward bow is rather straight forward. The large end can rotate within the socket of the fork blade to undo the bow, but this will throw off the orientation of the dropout. Simply un-braze, reorient, and re-braze the dropout to compensate for the new position of the fork blade.

4. Acquire new fork blades and try again.

Chapter 13: Cutting the Large Ends of the Fork Blades

Considerations and Pitfalls

Cutting from the large ends of the fork blades (as opposed to cutting mostly from the small ends) results in a supple fork with good vibration damping characteristics. Even if the builder wants a stiffer fork and cuts from the small ends, sometimes an additional small cut from the large end is necessary to fine tune the crown-to-axle length of the fork because the estimation method presented in Chapter 10 can lack precision for forks with large rakes. The two fork blade dropout subassemblies must have the same length after cutting and filing. A disparity greater than 1 mm complicates fork alignment.

Procedure for Cutting the Large Ends of the Fork Blades

1. At this stage, the fork blade dropout subassemblies should fit into their sockets on the crown as a result of step 3 of *Procedure for Brazing the Dropouts onto the Fork Blades*, Chapter 11. With an abrasive, remove the *S* or *L* marks from the blades that may remain if you cut the blades at the small ends (Chapter 10). Place your blades into your crown, making sure the blades are inserted all the way into the sockets.
2. On a level surface, lay the fork on one side. Using a tape measure placed along one side of the fork, measure from the middle of the slot to the bottom of the crown race (Figure 13-1). Record this number as the *precut crown-to-axle length*.

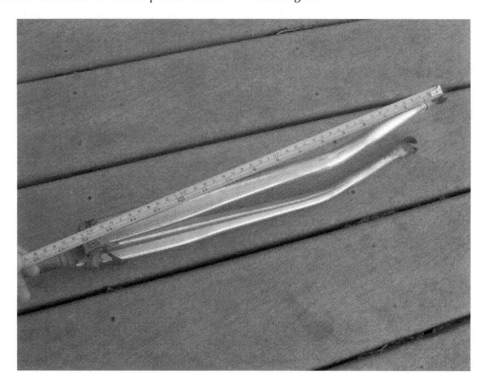

Figure 13-1: *Measuring the precut crown-to-axle length from the center of the slot to just below the crown race*

3. Subtract your desired crown-to-axle length from the precut crown-to-axle length obtained from step 2 above. The result is the *large-end cut*, an estimate of the amount of fork blade that needs to be removed to result in the desired crown-to-axle length. For example, if your precut crown-to-axle length is 425 mm and your desired crown-to-axle length is 400mm, your large-end cut will be: 425 mm – 400 mm = 25 mm.

4. Remove the fork blades from their sockets and place one on a level surface, outer side facing up. Measure along the long axis of the blade and mark the location of the large end cut (Figure 13-2).

Figure 13-2: *Measuring and marking the location of the large-end cut on the fork blade. In this example, we want our cut at 25 mm.*

5. Place the steering tube cutting guide on the fork blade so that the large-end cut mark lies in the cutting slot. Tighten the clamp down to secure the blade in place (Figure 13-3).

Figure 13-3: *The steering tube cutting guide clamped onto the fork blade. The large-end cut mark should lie in the cutting slot.*

6. Place the guide in your vise and cut from the large end of the fork blade with a hacksaw. The guide helps to ensure the cut occurs at ninety degrees to the fork blade's long axis. If you do not have a steering tube cutting guide, place the fork blade directly in the vise so that the cut mark lies just outside one of the ends of the jaws. Try to make your freehand cut as perpendicular as possible to the long axis of the fork blade.

7. On a level surface, lay down the cut fork blade on top of the uncut blade, aligning the two dropouts and long axes of the large ends. Trace onto the uncut blade the location of the cut mark (Figure 13-4).

Figure 13-4: *Lay the cut blade on top of the uncut blade and trace onto the uncut blade the location of the cut.*

8. Cut the uncut blade following steps 5 and 6 above.
9. Placed the two cut blades next to one another, aligning the long axes of the large ends and the dropouts. More likely than not, one blade will be longer than the other by a few millimeters. Mark the shorter blade with an *S*.
10. Inspect the cut large end of the *S* blade. Usually the cut will not be perfectly square, meaning the cut is not parallel to the cross section and/or not at a ninety degree angle to the long axis. If you used a steering tube cutting guide, usually the cut will be at a ninety degree angle to the long axis but not completely parallel to the cross section. If you cut the blade freehanded, usually the cut is neither perpendicular to the long axis nor parallel to the cross section. Touch up the end with a file until the end is square (Figure 13-5).

Figure 13-5: *In this example, we previously used a cutting guide to cut the large end of this fork blade. As a consequence, the cut is at ninety degrees to the long axis but not completely parallel to the cross section. The top surface on the right side of the fork blade is higher than the left. Filing can bring the right side down even with the left.*

11. Inspect the cut end of the longer blade. If needed, file the cut square as described in step 10.
12. Compare the two blade lengths again as described in step 9. Mark the longer blade with an *L*. Depending on how square the initials cuts were, it is possible that the *S* blade is now the *L* blade.
13. File the large end of the *L* blade using the flat surface of a file and applying even pressure to the entire cross section. This technique will help to preserve the square-ness of the large end as you filed it down. Stop periodically to compare the blade lengths, and continue filing until the two blade lengths are identical.
14. Attempt to insert the fork blades into their sockets in the crown. If, while making preparations to braze on the dropouts, you had to deform the large ends of the fork blades in the vise to make them fit into the crown (step 3, *Procedure for Brazing the Dropouts onto the Fork Blades*, Chapter 11), you may have to repeat this process because you have just cut off the deformed ends. If you only grinded out the insides of the sockets, the newly cut ends of the fork blades will probably fit the sockets without difficulty. Make adjustments if necessary.
15. Place your fork blades into their sockets in the crown. Place your front wheel in the dropouts (Figure 13-6). If the wheel is not centered between the blades, either one fork blade is longer than the other or the two fork blade sockets do not point out at the same angle. Usually, blade length discrepancy is the culprit. The wheel will be closer to the longer blade. Remove the wheel from the dropouts and the blades from their sockets.

Correct the underlying problem. Reassemble the fork. Place the wheel into the dropouts, and re-inspect the alignment. Repeat this troubleshooting process as necessary until the wheel is centered (Figure 13-7).

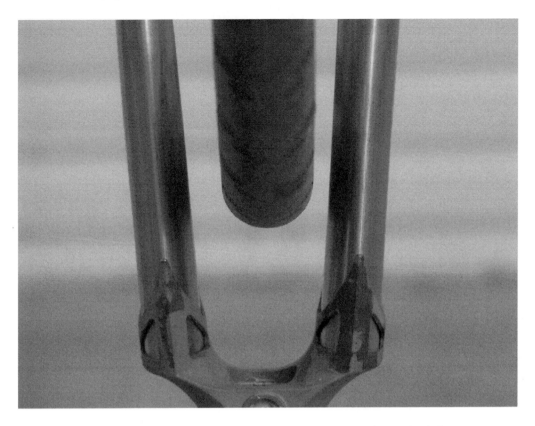

Figure 13-6: *The fork blade on the right is 1mm longer than the fork blade on the left. As a consequence, the wheel is un-centered and closer to the fork blade on the right.*

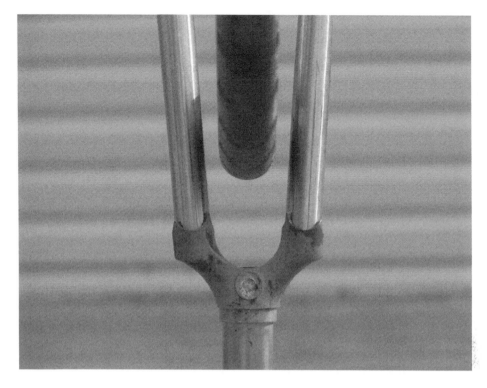

Figure 13-7: *A wheel centered in the fork blades. The two fork blades have the same length.*

Chapter 14: Brazing the Fork Blades into the Crown

Considerations and Pitfalls

In the past, I have owned a few imported mid-level production forks that came out of the box with less than ideal alignment. Surprisingly, the effect this sub-optimal alignment had on steering and handling was not noticeable. A properly aligned fork is, however, a mark of good craftsmanship.

Proper fork alignment occurs when the builder achieves four goals:

1. The wheel is centered between the fork blades.
2. The midline of the rim of the wheel aligns with the midline of the steering tube.
3. The wheel axle is parallel to the wide axis of the fork crown.
4. The distance between the insides of the dropouts corresponds to the OLD measurement of the front hub.

Equal fork blade lengths and rakes and proper placement of the fork blades into the crown during brazing are of paramount importance to achieve proper fork alignment. Some sort of jigging apparatus is also essential. A builder with limited resources can use a front wheel as an improvised fixture. The front wheel should be true, properly dished, and preferably not expensive as heat from brazing may damage the rim. A threaded rod can also be used as an improvised fixture in place of a front wheel. A front rack block with a quick release skewer, such as the *Hollywood Rack T970 Fork Block* allows more rapid jig assembly and disassembly than a threaded rod

A MAPP-air torch can be used to braze in the fork blades if the wall thickness of the fork blade sockets is 1.3 mm or thinner. Crowns with sloping shoulders are more likely to meet this requirement than flat top crowns. If the fork blade socket walls are thicker than 1.3 mm, an oxy-fuel torch is necessary to reach brazing temperature and achieve adequate penetration of filler alloy.

Even with professional quality jigs, forks often require cold setting to achieve proper alignment. The term *cold setting* is simply a euphemism for bending with a lever arm. Cold setting procedures are described in this chapter.

Procedure for Brazing the Fork Blades into the Crown Using a Fork Block

1. Place the fork blades into their sockets in the fork crown. Inspect the sockets and make a mental note of any socket points or edges that are not flush with the contours of the fork blades. On the inside of each fork blade, mark the location of the sockets point. Remove the fork blades.
2. Place one of your fork blades in your vise, inside facing up. Drill a small (3mm or 1/8" or smaller) gas vent hole at a location 1 cm below the mark made in step 1. The hole should extend through the inner wall of the fork blade but not through the outer wall. Without a gas vent hole, expanding gases can cause your fork blade to move during the brazing process, resulting in poor fork alignment.
3. Repeat step 2 with the opposite fork blade.

4. Use pliers to bend down any uneven points or edges of the fork crown's sockets (identified from step 1 above) flush with the fork blades.
5. Clean the outside and inside of the large ends of the fork blades and the fork blade sockets of the crown.
6. Apply a liberal amount of flux to the fork crown and the large ends of the fork blades.
7. Insert the fork blades into their sockets of the crown.
8. Place the fork block into the dropouts so that the flat portion of the block is at the front of the fork. Tighten down the quick release skewer (Figure 14-1). Try to wiggle the fork blades within their sockets. If they wiggle freely, remove them and tighten the fit by bending the socket edges and points inward with long nose pliers.

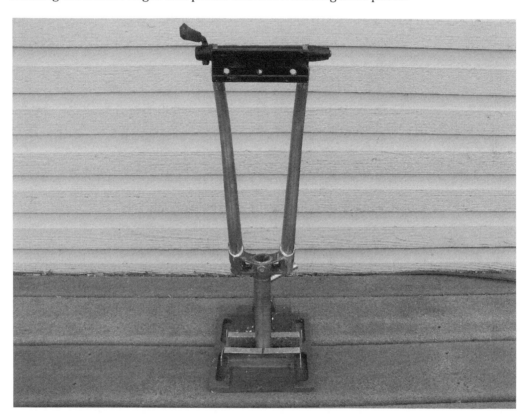

Figure 14-1: *Fork block used as a jig to secure the fork blades in place.*

9. Place the fork onto a flat surface (such as a sturdy piece of sheet metal) so that the flat portion of the tube block lies flush with the surface (Figure 14-2).
10. View the fork from the top. Measure the distance from the right most corner of the front of the fork crown to the top of your level surface (Figure 14-2). Repeat this measurement with the left most corner of the fork crown. If the two measurements differ by more than a millimeter, loosen or remove the fork block and pull the dropout with the shorter measurement forward (or the dropout with the longer measurement backward). Retighten the fork block and repeat the measurements described in this step. Repeat adjustments and measurements until you are satisfied with the results.

Figure 14-2: *Measuring from the front of the fork crown to the top of your level surface. This step helps ensure that the wheel axle runs parallel to the wide axis of the fork crown.*

11. Place the fork in your vise so that the dropouts point upward (Figure 14-1).
12. Braze the fork blades into their sockets.
13. Allow the fork to cool.
14. Remove your fork from the vise and the fork block from the dropouts.
15. Clean the fork crown with hot water and, if necessary, a wire brush and toilet bowl cleaner.

Procedure for Brazing the Fork Blades into the Crown Using a Wheel

1. Perform steps 1 through 7 of *Procedure for Brazing the Fork Blades into the Crown Using a Fork Block* (above).
2. Place your front wheel in the dropouts, but clamp down the quick release skewer only partway. You should be able to wiggle the fork blades within their sockets.
3. Place the end of the steering tube in the vise so that the fork is oriented upside down.
4. Place the inclinometer along the side of the steering tube. Move the fork within the vise until the inclinometer indicates the steering tube is perpendicular to the ground. (Essentially this is the same step as the one depicted in Figure 9-2 [top], Chapter 9, only this time the fork blades are in their sockets).
5. Push and pull the dropouts, from front to back and from side to side, until the wheel axle appears parallel to the wide axis of the crown and the rim is centered between the fork blades. Place the inclinometer on the side of the rim to make sure the plane of the wheel is perpendicular to the ground (Figure 14-3). You should be able to achieve these alignment parameters if you followed the procedures in the previous chapters correctly. If not,

disassemble your subassemblies to figure out what is amiss. The most likely culprit is a disparity in the lengths or rakes of the two fork blades. Correct the problem and continue. When the fork appears appropriately aligned, clamp down the quick release skewer tightly.

Figure 14-3: *When using a wheel as an improvised fixture, use an inclinometer along the rim at the front of the wheel to make sure the plane of the wheel lies perpendicular to the steering tube.*

6. Braze the fork blades into their sockets. To avoid ruining your wheel, try to focus the flame away from the rim.
7. Allow the fork to cool. Remove your wheel from the fork and the fork from the vise.
8. Clean the fork crown with hot water and, if necessary, a wire brush and toilet bowl cleaner.

Procedure for Brazing the Fork Blades into the Crown Using a Threaded Rod

1. Perform steps 1 through 7 of *Procedure for Brazing the Fork Blades into the Crown Using a Fork Block* (above).
2. Place the dummy axle you created for the procedure in Chapter 11 into your dropouts. Place a nut on the outside of each dropout and tighten down the two outermost nuts finger tight.
3. Place the steering tube of your fork in the vise so that the long axis is roughly parallel to the ground. Place your inclinometer on the front of your crown and rotate the steering tube within the vise until the front of the crown is parallel to the ground. (Figure 14-4). Tighten down the jaws of the vise so that the steering tube will not rotate or slip.

Figure 14-4: *Use your inclinometer to orient the front of the fork crown parallel to the ground.*

4. Place your inclinometer on your threaded rod and move the dropouts up or down until the threaded rod is parallel to the ground (Figure 14-5).

Figure 14-5: *Using an inclinometer to orient the threaded rod parallel to the ground and to the wide axis of the fork crown.*

5. Perform steps 3 and 4 of *Procedure for Brazing the Fork Blades into the Crown Using a Wheel* (above) to place your steering tube perpendicular to the ground. Be sure not to move the fork blades within their sockets as you orient the fork vertically.

6. Place the inclinometer on top of the threaded rod (Figure 14-6). Moving the dropouts side to side (and not from front to back), you should be able to find a location where the rod is parallel to the ground. If not, something is amiss. The most likely culprit is a disparity in the lengths or rakes of the two fork blades. Correct the problem and continue. When the rod is parallel to the ground. Tighten down the outside nuts onto the dropouts with a wrench.

Figure 14-6: *Using an inclinometer to orient the threaded rod parallel to the ground.*

7. Braze the fork blades into their sockets.
8. Allow your fork to cool. Remove your threaded rod from the fork and the fork from the vise.
9. Clean the fork crown with hot water and, if necessary, a wire brush and toilet bowl cleaner.

Procedure for Cold Setting the Dropouts

1. Place the steering tube in the vise so that the dropouts point upward.
2. Place the wheel in the dropouts but do not tighten down the quick release skewer.
3. Inspect the position of the rim relative to the two fork blades. If rim is centered or near centered between the blades (Figure 13-7, Chapter 13) proceed to step 4 below. If the rim is obviously off center and significantly closer to one blade (Figure 13-6, Chapter 13), proceed to *Procedure for Cold Setting the Fork Blades* and return to dropout alignment later.

4. Inspect one of your dropouts to determine how it lies relative to the outer surface of the wheel hub. If the inner surface of the dropout lies flush relative to the outer surface of the hub, no cold setting is required. If only the bottom surface of the dropout touches the hub, the dropout needs to be bent outward. If only the top surface of the dropout touches the hub, the dropout needs to be bent inward. (If the dropout is rotated, either the front or rear surface of the dropout touches the inner surface of the hub. I do not recommend the novice builder cold set a rotated dropout. If the rotation is severe, you will need to un-braze, realign, and re-braze the affected dropout).

5. Remove your fork from the vise.

6. Place the uncorrected dropout in the vise so that the vise jaws completely cover the slot (Figure 14-7).

7. Grab the end of the steering tube. To bend the dropout outward, push the fork away from you. To bend the dropout inward, pull the fork towards you. Over correction is surprisingly easy, so only make a small bend.

Figure 14-7: *Cold setting the dropouts. The entire slot must lie within the jaws of the vise or the builder risks making a bend within the dropout and not above it.*

8. Repeat steps 4 through 7 until you are satisfied with your dropout alignment.

9. Repeat steps 4 through 8 with the opposite dropout.

Procedure for Cold Setting the Fork Blades

1. Place the steering tube in the vise so that the dropouts point upward.
2. Measure the distance between the inner surfaces of the dropouts and compare the result to the OLD of your front hub. If you are within 2 mm of your target OLD, the dropout spacing need not be adjusted. If the measurement is 2 mm bigger than OLD, the dropout spacing should be made smaller. If the measurement is 2 mm smaller than OLD, the dropout spacing should be made bigger.
3. Place the wheel in the dropouts but do not tighten down the quick release skewer.
4. Inspect the position of the rim relative to the two fork blades. Determine if the rim is centered between the blades (Figure 13-7, Chapter 13) or offset (Figure 13-7, Chapter 13).
5. Formulate a strategy to correct your fork alignment problem. If the rim is acceptably centered but the spacing for OLD needs adjustment, both fork blades need to be moved either inward (if too wide) or outward (if too narrow). If spacing for OLD is acceptable but the rim is not centered, you will need to move the closer blade inward and the farther blade outward. If spacing for OLD and rim alignment are both problematic, first correct spacing for OLD by making adjustment to a single fork blade (as described above). Adjust the opposite fork blade only if your initial adjustment does not center the rim.
6. Remove the wheel from the fork blades.
7. Rotate the fork within the vise so that the wide axis of the crown runs perpendicular to the vise jaws (Figure 14-8).
8. Place a long hollow lever (such as the square tube used to bend the fork blades in Chapter 12) over a fork blade that needs adjusting (Figure 14-8). To move the fork blade inwards, push the lever away from you. To move the fork blade outwards, pull the lever towards you. Over correction is surprisingly easy, so only make a small bend.
9. Perform step 8 on the opposite fork blade (if necessary).
10. Measure the distance between the inner surfaces of the dropouts.
11. Place your wheel in the dropouts and check if the rim is centered.
12. Repeat steps 1 through 11 until you are satisfied with your alignment.

Figure 14-8: *Cold setting the fork blades with a long lever. The movement of the lever must occur perpendicular to the vise jaws or the fork will slide out of the vise.*

Chapter 15: Brake Mounts

Considerations and Pitfalls

Caliper brakes require a hole that completely transverses the walls of the steering tube and crown. At this point in the build, we have already drilled through the crown (Chapter 9) but we have not drilled through our steering tube. In this chapter, we complete the hole, drilling the rest of the way through the steering tube. Even if you do not want to use a caliper brake, completing the hole provides a location to mount lights, reflectors, fenders, or other bicycle parts. Modern caliper brakes use a recessed mounting nut, requiring different holes at the front and back of the fork. Usually the mounting bolt of the caliper is 6 mm in diameter, requiring a 6 mm hole at the front of the fork. The recessed mounting nut is usually 8 mm in diameter requiring an 8 mm hole at the back of the fork. If you plan to use an older style caliper with a standard hex nut rather than a recessed mounting nut, you should drill 6 mm holes at the front and back of the fork.

Metric drill bits are sometimes difficult to obtain at hardware stores in the US. A ¼" drill bit is 6.35 mm in diameter. A 6.35 mm hole is acceptable to mount bike parts such as fenders, lights, or reflectors. However, the 6 mm mounting bolt of a caliper brake will wobble loosely in a ¼" hole. If you cannot locate a 6 mm drill bit and want to mount caliper brakes, I recommend you drill out your hole to 3/16" (4.76 mm) and use a hand reamer to enlarge the hole to 6 mm. If you cannot locate a 6 mm drill bit and do not plan on mounting a caliper brake, enlarge the hole to ¼" (6.35 mm).

Cantilever brakes require cantilever brake bosses. Much like the fork blades, the two brake bosses must be properly aligned relative to one another. To obtain proper alignment, the builder will need to make a simple improvised fixture. Slight departures from ideal alignment (1 or 2 mm too high or too low or 1 to 2 degrees of rotation about the long axes the fork blades) have little effect on braking because the vast majority of cantilever brakes provide a mechanism to fine tune the location and angle of the brake pad. However, properly aligned brake bosses are a hallmark of good craftsmanship. Many builders use brass to braze on cantilever brake bosses because they are afraid that fillets formed from silver bearing brazing alloy are prone to failure. Were this concern unequivocally true, manufacturers would not supply stainless brake bosses, which require a silver-bearing alloy.

Having both a hole for caliper brakes and cantilever brake bosses allows the rider to pick and choose between different types of braking mechanisms. This set up is particularly useful if the rider intends to swap out between different rim sizes periodically.

Procedure for Drilling the Steering Tube

1. Place the steering tube in your vise so that the front of the fork faces upward. Clamp down the vise (Figure 15-1).
2. Place a few drops of cutting oil on the area to be drilled. Drill a small hole using a small (1/8" or 3 mm) titanium nitride bit, a slow drill speed setting, and firm downward pressure. If you cannot get the drill bit to bite, dimple the steering tube with a center punch. Flip the fork over and drill the back of the crown. Repeat the process with 4 mm, 5 mm, and 6 mm

(or ¼") bits until you can fit the 6 mm (or ¼") bit all the way through the steering tube (Figure 15-1). If you cannot find metric drill bits and wish to mount a caliper brake, do not drill beyond a 3/16" (4.76 mm) hole.

3. Attempt to fit your brake caliper mounting bolt through the front hole. If the hole is too narrow or burrs do not allow the bolt to completely penetrate your hole, use a hand reamer to ream out the hole slightly until the bolt fits (Figure 15-2).

Figure 15-1: *Drilling out the front of the steering tube. In this photograph, the builder is using a 6 mm drill bit to enlarge a 5 mm hole.*

Figure 15-2: *Use a hand reamer to ream out the hole until the 6mm bolt fits. A tight fit is better than a loose fit. The hand reamer can enlarge a 3/16" (4.76 mm) hole to a 6 mm hole if a 6mm drill bit is unavailable.*

4. If you want a 6 mm hole at the back of your fork, flip the fork over in the vise and repeat step 3 at the back of your crown. If you want an 8 mm hole for a recessed mounting nut, enlarge the hole with a larger drill bit and/or hand reamer until the recessed bolt fits snugly.

Procedure for Brazing on Cantilever Brake Bosses (Optional)

1. With an abrasive, clean the fork blades where you anticipate mounting the cantilever brake bosses. Give yourself a large margin for error, cleaning a larger area than seems necessary.
2. Place your wheel in the dropouts of your fork.
3. Adjust the pad on one of your cantilever brake arms so that the pad is mounted at an intermediate location and angle. This adjustment allows you a little bit of leeway in the event you mount your brake bosses slightly too high or too low.
4. Place the brake arm adjusted in step 3 above onto one of the brake bosses. Place the boss on the fork blade so that the brake pad contacts the rim (Figure 15-3). Adjust the mounting location of the brake pad within the caliper if the caliper does not appear to lie at a functional angle relative to the long axis of the fork blade. Mark on the blade the top and bottom locations of the brake boss (Figure 15-3).
5. Measure downward from a conspicuous location on the fork crown, such as a socket point, to the two marks made in step 4 above. Record these measurements.
6. On the opposite side of the fork, place the end of the tape measure at a location on the crown congruent to your measuring point from step 5 above. On the blade, mark at the two

distances you recorded from step 5 (Figure 15-4). These marks represent the future top and bottom locations of your other brake boss.

Figure 15-3: *Marks representing the top and bottom locations of the brake boss.*

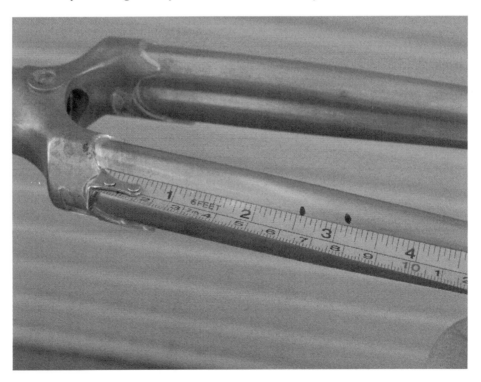

Figure 15-4: *On the other fork blade, mark the locations corresponding to the top and bottom of the remaining brake boss.*

7. Obtain a rigid strip of aluminum approximately 3 mm (1/8") thick, 150 mm long and 15 mm wide. No special grade of aluminum is required. Simply purchase the correct gauge from a hardware store or metal fabrication shop and cut off a strip at the appropriate length and width.

8. Drill a 6 mm or ¼" hole at one end of your aluminum strip.

9. Place the aluminum strip onto the front of your fork blades over the marks made in steps 4 through 6 above. Place the hole made in step 8 at the inside edge of one fork blade. Make a 2 to 3 cm long mark on the aluminum strip at the end opposite the hole. This mark should extend inward from the center of the fork blade (Figure 15-5).

10. Place your aluminum strip in your vise and drill 6 mm (or ¼") holes at the two ends of the mark made in step 9 above. If the two holes do not intersect, drill a third (or even fourth) hole between the first two. Using a rotary tool with a grinding bit, grind the inside edges of the intersecting holes until you have an oblong oval shape (Figure 15-6). A 6 mm bolt should be able to slide completely back and forth within the oval.

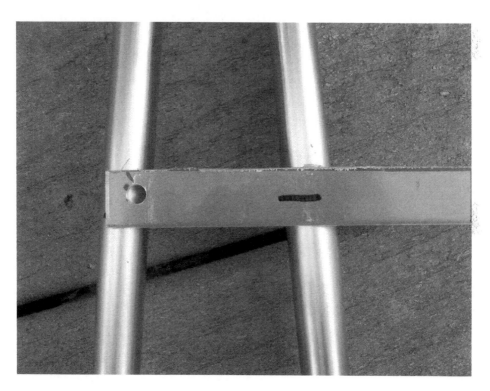

Figure 15-5: *Preparing the brake boss jig. The aluminum strip should lie on the fork blades over the marks corresponding to the tops and bottoms of the brake bosses.*

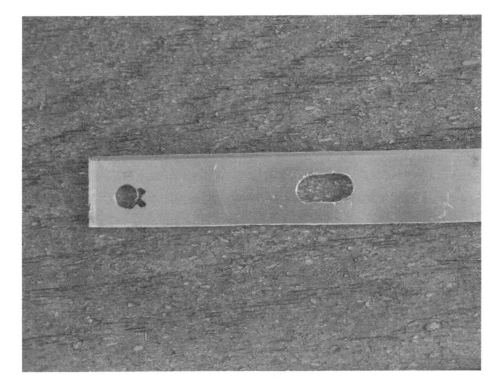

Figure 15-6: *Finished brake boss fixture. The oval hole on the right side allows one of the bosses to slide back and forth, fine tuning fit to the correct location.*

11. Clean the brake bosses with an abrasive.
12. Place the steering tube of your fork in the vise so that the front of the fork faces upward.
13. Bolt the brake bosses loosely into your brake boss jig. The small holes in the bosses that take the ends of the calipers' tension springs will need to be on the inner sides of the fork blades (Figure 15-7).
14. Flux the brake bosses and the front of the fork blades.
15. Place the brake-bosses-jig assembly onto the front of the fork blades. You will need to rotate the bosses upon their bolts and move the boss bolted to the oval hole of the jig from side to side until the bosses line up with the marks made in steps 4 through 6 (above) and the mitered contours of the bosses have maximum overlap with the fork blades. Tighten down the bolts of the jig to preserve this orientation (Figure 15-7).

Figure 15-7: *Gravity and the brake boss jig hold the brake bosses in the correct location and orientation during brazing. The small holes in the brake bosses that secure the ends of the calipers' tension springs should lie on the inner sides of the fork blades.*

16. Braze your brake bosses in place. The walls of the brake bosses are thicker than the walls of the fork blades, so focus the flame primarily onto the bosses. Build up a small fillet of brazing alloy between each boss and fork blade (Figure 15-8).
17. Allow the bosses to cool. Remove the jig. Clean the brazed area with hot water and, if necessary, a wire brush and toilet bowl cleaner.

Figure 15-8: *A fillet of brazing alloy (lighter colored metal) reinforces the joint between the brake boss and fork blade.*

Chapter 16: Cutting the Crown Race

Considerations and Pitfalls

The crown race cutting tool reduces the diameter of the fork crown race so that the headset race ring can fit tightly around the steering tube. The race cutter also faces the top surface of the crown so that the race ring sits perpendicular to the steering tube.

The outside diameter of the fork crown race should be 0.05 to 0.15 mm wider than the inside diameter of the headset crown race, resulting in a tight press fit. A loose fitting headset crown race ring can lead to premature wear of the headset bearings as well as a noisy clicking sound often indistinguishable from the noise of a loose bottom bracket cartridge. An improperly faced crown can result in a tilted headset crown race ring, a poorly fitting headset, and pitting or premature wear of the headset bearings.

The outer diameter of an uncut fork crown race is typically 27.1 mm for crowns that take a 25.4 mm steering tube. Common headset race ring inner diameters are 26.4, 26.5, and 27.0 mm for 25.4 mm steering tubes. The race ring inner diameter is typically 30.0 mm for 28.6 mm steering tubes. The blades of a crown race cutting tool are not adjustable. Cutting ends are specific to a single diameter crown race.

Bicycle shops charge between $15 and $30 to cut a fork crown race. The mechanic will need to know the diameter of your headset race ring. Not all bicycle shops perform this service. You can skip the procedure below if the local bike shop cuts your crown race.

There are three major methods to secure a fork during the crown race cutting process:

1. The builder can bolt a fork block to a sturdy workbench and clamp the dropouts of the fork into the block.
2. The builder can place the short axis of the fork crown in the vise so that the steering tube lies parallel to the ground.
3. The builder can place a wheel in the dropouts of the fork and secure the wheel between his legs while he cuts with his hands. A rag placed on top of the wheel can protect the tire from metal shards.

Procedure for Cutting the Crown Race (Optional)

1. Secure your fork using one of the three methods described above.
2. Place the appropriate blade onto the handle of your crown race cutting tool.
3. Apply a liberal amount of cutting oil to your fork crown race and the blade of your cutting tool.
4. Place the crown race cutting tool over your steering tube (Figure 16-1).

Figure 16-1: *When cutting the crown race, the tool must be rotated clockwise.*

5. Cut by applying downward pressure while moving the handles of the tool clockwise. Never turn the tool counterclockwise.
6. Periodically, lift up the blade and inspect the crown race to assess your progress. Scores of tool rotations are required to reach the top surface of the fork crown. Reapply cutting oil regularly.
7. When you reach the top of the crown, continue cutting for an additional 5 to 10 rotations. The top of the crown should be faced flat (Figure 16-2).

Figure 16-2: *The top of the fork crown after cutting the crown race. Note how the top surface of the fork has been faced flat and how the 26.4mm crown race is only slightly wider than the 25.4mm steering tube above.*

Troubleshooting

Inexpensive crown race cutting tools that do not have blades within the tool's bore can cut the crown race too narrow. In the event the race ring fits the crown race loosely, the builder can effectively knurl the crown race to raise its outer diameter with several dozen small pits created with a center punch. Red thread locking compound can also help to secure a race ring to a knurled crown race.

Chapter 17: Painting

Final Clean Up

Remove all rust, scale, residual brazing flux, and dirt using a metal brush, toilet bowl cleaner, or abrasives until all surfaces are bright and shiny. You can remove shallow tool marks left by files, cutting blades, and grinding bits by sanding. Sandpaper with 60 to 120 grit works well. Deep tool marks are best left in place because excess sanding can leave steel walls thin and weak. Painting will make deep tool marks less conspicuous. Excess brazing alloy at the shorelines of lugs can be smoothed down with needle files. When clean, you should thoroughly rinse down your fork with water. Dry the fork as soon as possible with a clean rag to prevent the buildup of rust.

The Rattle Can Paint Job

The term *rattle can* applies to spray paint available in canisters that rattle when shaken. Although inexpensive, most spray paint that comes in disposable cans chips and scratches very easily and is not very durable. Engine enamels, which are offered at some automobile parts supply stores, offer enhanced scratch resistance but are not nearly as durable as a professional powder coat. Never apply an enamel color coat over a lacquer primer.

If you wish to paint your fork yourself, you should acquire string or wire, one can of primer, and one canister of the desired final color. After thoroughly cleaning the fork, you should mask the crown race and the ends of the brake bosses with masking tape. Mask the steering tube with old newspaper (Figure 17-1). You should tie a section of the wire or string around a washer with an outer diameter larger than the inner diameter of your steering tube (Figure 17-1). To suspend the fork from an overhang, thread the wire or string through the steering tube so that the bottom of the crown rests on the washer.

Detailed directions for spray painting are written on the outside of spray cans. In short, you should apply three coats of primer with a ten minute pause between each coat. When spray painting, you should use smooth even strokes. If you point the nozzle at a single point for a prolonged period, the paint will likely run or bleb at that location. If you jerk the can or move it too rapidly, you will create an aerosol cloud. Small aerosol droplets of paint will adhere to the fork and the resulting paint job will have a gritty texture. Sanding is optional. For enamel paints, a seven day duration is required for the primer to cure before applying a colored layer of paint.

For the colored layer of paint, apply three or four coats of paint with a ten minute pause between each coat. Generally, multiple thin coats create a better final appearance than fewer thick coats. Blebs and runs sometimes smooth out spontaneously during the curing process. Sanding is optional. Clear coating is also optional but can increase durability and chip resistance. For enamel paints, a seven day duration is required for the colored layer to cure before applying a clear coat.

Chips and scratches in rattle can paint jobs are inevitable. You can touch up the paint job by spraying paint onto a piece of cardboard and by using a small paintbrush or cotton swab to transfer the paint onto the fork. If the chip goes down to bare metal, you will need to first paint the scratch with primer and later paint with the final color.

Figure 17-1: *Masking the crown race and steering tube prior to painting. By threading the string and washer through the bottom of the steering tube, you can suspend the fork from an overhang while spray painting.*

The Professional Paint Job using Liquid Paint

Automotive enamel paint is durable and available in thousands of colors. Some automobile painting businesses will paint a bicycle fork. Custom bicycle frame and fork painting businesses also exist and usually advertise online.

For liquid paint, I recommend the builder incorporate the crown and socketed dropouts into the aesthetic of the frame rather than hide the lugs with a single, solid color paint job. A common two color theme for a lugged fork is to paint the crown and dropouts one color and the blades another. The cost of a professional paint job for a single fork is highly variable.

The Professional Powder Coat

During powder coating, tiny beads of plastic are sprayed onto the fork and adhere through electrostatic forces. The coaters bake the fork, melting the tiny beads into a single plastic outer coat. This coat is extremely durable. Powder coats generally occur as a single, solid color (Figure 17-2). To preserve the artistic detail of the lugged crown and socketed dropouts, thin coats are preferable to thicker coats.

You will need to explain to the powder coater the areas of the fork that need to be masked off. Preferably, you should find a powder coater that routinely paints bicycle frames and forks. Powder coat that adheres onto inappropriate locations, such as the ends of brake bosses or the crown race, is difficult to remove.

Generally, powder coaters have a minimum cost of $70 to $100 for their services to cover setup expenses. For common colors, such as gloss black, some coaters will allow you to piggy back a small job onto someone else's larger order for a small fee.

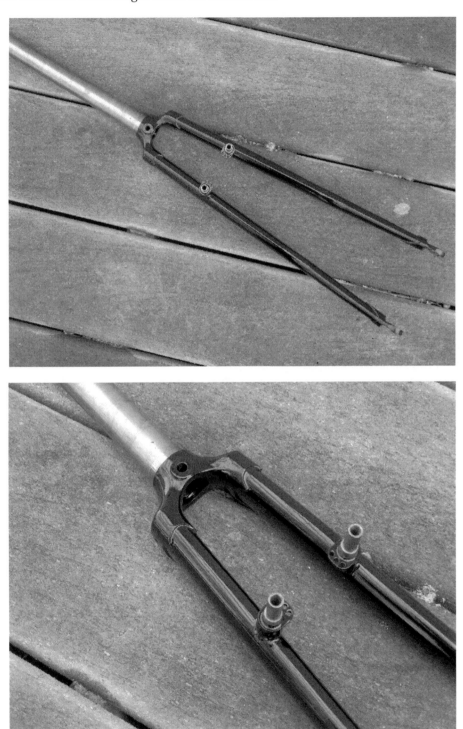

Figure 17-2: *Appearance of a bicycle fork after a glossy black powder coat.*

Chapter 18: Recommended Reading and Other Resources

Books and Other Print

1. Chimonas, Marc-Andre R. (2013). *Lugged Bicycle Frame Construction. Third Edition.* Seattle, USA: Createspace.
2. Paterek, Tim (2004). *The Paterek Manual For Bicycle Framebuilders, Shop Edition.* Portland, USA: Tim Paterek.
3. Cain, Tubal (2008). *Soldering and Brazing, Workshop Practice Series Number 9.* Norfolk, UK: Special Interest Model Books.
4. Sloane, Eugene A. (1995). *Sloane's Complete Book of Bicycling.* New York, USA: Simon & Schuster.
5. Heine, Jan, et al. (2005). *The Golden Age of Handbuilt Bicycles.* Seattle, USA: Vintage Bicycle Press.
6. Finch, Richard (2007). *Welder's Handbook.* Berkley, USA: Berkley Publishing Group.
7. Schwartz, Mel (1995). *Brazing for the Engineering Technologist.* New York, USA: Chapman & Hall.
8. Rossman, Hahn, et al. (2011). "An Overview of Frame Geometry." *Bicycle Quarterly Vol. 10 No 2.* Seattle, USA: Bicycle Quarterly Press.

Online Fork and Frame Building Supplies

1. Nova Cycles Supply Inc. (2012). Available at URL: http://www.novacycles.com/catalog/. Last accessed 24 February 2012.
2. Bikelugs.com (2012). Available at URL: http://www.bikelugs.com/. Last accessed 24 February 2012.
3. Henry James Bicycles (2012). Available at URL: http://www.henryjames.com/. Last accessed 24 February 2012.
4. Ceeway Bike Building Supplies (2012). Available at URL: http://www.ceeway.com/. Last accessed 24 February 2012.
5. Fairing Industrial Inc. (2012). Available at URL: http://www.fairing.com/. Last accessed 24 February 2012.
6. Bringheli Frames-Tools & Jigs (2012). Available at URL: http://www.bringheli.com/. Last accessed 24 February 2012.
7. Paragon Machine Works (2012). Available at URL: http://www.paragonmachineworks.com/. Last accessed 8 April 2012.

Brazing Supplies

1. Airgas, Gas, Welding, Safety Supply (2012). Available at URL: http://www.airgas.com/. Last accessed 24 February 2012.
2. Harbor Freight Tools (2012). Available at URL: http://www.harborfreight.com/. Last accessed 24 February 2012.
3. The Harris Products Group (2012). Available at URL: http://www.harrisproductsgroup.com/. Last accessed 8 April 2012.

Feedback and Technical Support

Having problems building your fork? Need a copy of the spreadsheet that contains the calculations described in Chapter 5: Quantitative Bicycle Fork Design? Do you wish to share a complaint or compliment with the editorial staff or author? Visit our website at http://luggedbicycle.weebly.com/technical-support.html to contact us.

About the Author

Marc-Andre R. Chimonas learned the fundamentals of technical writing as a student at Georgia Tech and as an officer in the US Epidemic Intelligence Service. He is the author of *Lugged Bicycle Frame Construction* and the electronic pulp novel *Magic Sky Daddy*. He has published articles in *Boneshaker: A Bicycling Almanac* and various peer-reviewed medical science journals.

Notes

Notes

Notes

Notes

Notes

Notes

Notes

Notes

Manufactured by Amazon.ca
Bolton, ON